HAMISH HENDERSON

Collected Poems and Songs

Edited by
Raymond Ross

Curly Snake Publishing

Ladyis…

This is the legend of my life, though Latyne it be nane

Acknowledgements

Some of the poems and songs published here have appeared previously in *Ballads of World War II* (The Lili Marleen Club of Glasgow, Glasgow, 1949); *Broadsheet* magazine (Dublin and Edinburgh); *Cencrastus* magazine (Edinburgh); *Chapman* magazine (Edinburgh); *Elegies for the Dead in Cyrenaica* (John Lehmann, London 1948, EUSPB, Edinburgh 1977, Polygon 1990); *The End of a Regime?* (AUP, Aberdeen, 1991); *Englische Lyrik 1900-1980* (Reclam, Leipzig, 1983); *Favourite Scottish Song Lyrics* (Gordon Wright, Edinburgh, 1983); *Homage to John MacLean* (John MacLean Society, Larkhall, 1973); *Lines Review* magazine (Loanhead); *Modern Folk Ballads* (Studio Vista, London ,1966); *No Other Place* (Tuckwell Press, East Linton ,1995); *Oasis* magazine (Cairo); *The Obscure Voice* (Morning Star, Edinburgh, 1994); *Pervigilium Scotiae: Tom Scott, Somhairle MacGill-Eain, Hamish Henderson, etruscan reader II* (etruscan books, Buckfastleigh, 1997); *The People's Past* (EUSPB, Edinburgh, 1980); *Poems of the Second World War: the Oasis Selection* (Dent, London 1985, 1995); *Poems to Hugh MacDiarmid* (Akros, Preston, 1967); *Poeti della Scozia Contemporanea* (Supernova, Venice, 1992); *Poetry of War 1939-1945* (New English Library, London, 1972); *Poetry of the World Wars* (London, 1990); *Poetry Scotland* magazine; *The Rebels Ceilidh Song Book* (Bo'ness Rebels Literary Society, Bo'ness, 1951); *The Ring of Words* (Oliver and Boyd, Edinburgh, 1970); *Scotland's Music* (Mainstream/BBC Scotland, Edinburgh, 1992); *Scottish Verse 1851-1951* (Nelson, Edinburgh 1952); *The Voice of Scotland* magazine.

All poems & notes copyright © Hamish Henderson 2000

Introduction © Raymond Ross

Cover design & illustration © Fred Crayk

Design & typesetting by Richard Kealey

Sheet music "Auld Reekie's Roses" courtesy of Hayden Murphy *Broadsheet*
All other sheet music by R.W. Palmer courtesy of etruscan books

Curly Snake Publishing
Unit One
Abbeymount Techbase
Easter Road
Edinburgh
EH8 8EJ

THE SCOTTISH ARTS COUNCIL

Introduction

These collected poems and songs of Hamish Henderson, one of the great figures of 20th century Scotland, have been arranged in this volume with regard to the time at which they were written and to the sometimes momentous events in the poet's life which they evoke.

In this way it is hoped that the poems and songs will reflect the 'legend' of both the poet's individual life and the times through which he has lived, capturing both the 'inner' or spiritual and 'outer' or experiential life of the poet simultaneously.

With regard to the poet's Second World War experiences, for example, a poem like "Ballad of the Simeto", begun in war-time Sicily where it is 'set', but not completed until after the war, is placed *in medias res*, in the midst of things, as we follow the poet's journey "to Sicily, to Sicily / over the dark moving waters" as he bids farewell to the desert war.

Similarly, the *Elegies*, though not completed until 1947 and not published until 1948, and which were begun in Africa and worked on throughout the war years, are placed accordingly before the poems and songs which evoke the poet's later experiences and memories of both the Sicilian and Italian campaigns.

This retrospective immediacy is an attempt to let the poems breathe where we think they belong and from where they can resonate most powerfully.

Many of the poems are previously unpublished or have only been partially published to date in written form. It being the long held belief of a poet steeped in the oral tradition that the first speaking of a poem – or the singing of a song – counts as much towards publication as its first appearance in print, this cultural imperative has also had a bearing on the structure of the volume.

"Glasclune and Drumlochy", a poem which includes a song, for example, was begun before the war and does evoke the poet's Perthshire childhood, but this one had a long gestation and was finally launched as a spoken poem "around 1960" which is where we locate it because, as a folk-poem, it was very much part of the Folk Revival in Scotland (and not published in print for another two decades).

Other poems which have received no public airing to date, whether in print or from the lips of the poet himself, have also been arranged according to this round chronology.

Some of the soldier ballads, published here under the poet's name for the first time, appeared anonymously – or at least as "collected by" Hamish Henderson in the guise of Seumas Mor MacEanruig in *Ballads of World War II*, a private publication aimed to defeat the censorship of the day. Others are seeing print for the first time.

Some songs, in fact, began life as poems before being put to music. This is one of the reasons why there is no segregation of songs from poems. The poetic qualities of songs like "Auld Reekie's Roses" or "The Freedom Come All Ye" hardly need stressing; and any print demarcation which would, in effect, incarcerate the songs in a different section, would go against the spirit of Henderson's life and work as creator, collector and cultural catalyst. The names of tunes are supplied and, in some instances, the musical score is provided.

Nor do we make any distinction between barrack-room or soldier ballads and those with a more obvious 'literary' distinction. They are all part of the same man, the same cultural commitment.

On the same note, Dr Henderson's translations of poems have not been subject to any cultural apartheid process which would relegate them to a township or ghetto of their own. This is for several reasons. A good translation, arguably, is a poem in its own right. But also, by placing them in the main body of the text, the translation poems not only demonstrate the breadth of the poet's European heritage, they also display particular influences on and abiding concerns of the writer. This too informs the legend of our days as seen through the eyes of the poet.

In the past Dr Henderson often declared, when pressed by others to make more of his own poetry, that he had put all his "eggs in the one basket", referring to his commitment to the Folk Revival, of which he is undoubtedly the father figure in Scotland. Hence, and with characteristic modesty, he was often blate (as opposed to late) when it came to publishing his own poems.

Through his work at the School of Scottish Studies, as a collector, balladeer and instigator of the Folk Revival, as well as in his unceasing efforts for such causes as Scottish Home Rule, the anti-apartheid and nuclear disarmament movements, and for a democratic socialism (though, in their historical phase, Stalinist tendencies, gentle reader, are apparent!) Henderson has made Scotland an immensely richer place. But, without a proper recognition of the poet Henderson, Scotland would still have remained very much the poorer.

Hamish Henderson is one of the most interesting, not to say outstanding, voices of 20th century Scotland; and his poetry, by its very nature, evokes much that is vital to Scottish and European history, society and culture.

These are poems of lyrical intensity and gentle humour, of subtle irony and satirical intent, of profound humanity and, on occasion, of cold steel. Henderson writes with fire in his belly and love in his heart of war and peace, of the Highland, urban and desert landscapes, of the footslogging swaddie and the resistance hero, of childhood memories and erotic encounters, of pain, love, regret and death. And of hope.

But perhaps the underlying and unifying concern is faith: faith in ordinary humanity to pull through whatever the odds. Of the many outstanding 20th century poets Scotland has produced, it is perhaps Henderson, above all the others, who gives voice to that ordinary humanity in its quest for survival and for better days.

Raymond Ross
Editor
At the Sign of the Curly Snake
Edinburgh, January 2000

Contents

Auldearn

Amorous Hornie summons to his dance
long-buried elders sure of their election:
and glowering clouds advance.

The bells foretell no woodland resurrection
no sticky-eyed awakening among midges.
                    The unholy manse
slavers afternoon terrors under the hill.
While black man Clootie crawls among fern-scruffed ridges
the hairy witch sits on the window-sill.

Inverey

Over the low hills gropes a muffled hate
With slouch hat over brow and eyes - dark eyes
Sightlessly cruel in the intricate ways.
No lightening soon or late.

Song

(adapted from Horace)

Vivamus mea Lesbia atque amemus

Nou Jeannie dear, ye mauna fear
      the rants o dour auld bodies O.
Ye're daft to miss a single kiss
      to please sic muckle cuddies O.

We havenae lang for "luve's sweet sang" –
      It's shair the morn's the deil's O.
He'll douse the licht, an' lea in nicht
      the waltzes an' quadrilles O!

Sae kiss me mair, ma carrot-hair,
      a thousan kisses gie me O.
(But dinna count the hale amount
      lest Dick an' Denny see me O)

Love Song

(to a Highland air)

I'll always be waiting
Where streams are afore me.
A silly sun is lighting
The clock that ticks surely
And others desire me.
But seven streams with leaping
To one love will keep me,
For loneliness arm me.

I'll always be waiting
Where Linnhe lies under
And mountains are beating
The long loch with thunder
Its waters rain-fleeting.
But thoughts can never fley me.
There's killing and fighting
But soon ye'll be near me.

And I'll aye be waiting
Where streams are afore me.

Bridge St Blues

I was reading Malherbe
        and your smile came into my mind,
So I left Malherbe
        and his starchy verse behind.
I put on a mac; then I paused
        and I grinced with pain.
From one end of this town to the other
        I walked in the rain.
I knew what I'd say when I found you.
        It's quite absurd.
You smiled and I stammered
        a totally different word.

This is the road
        now blocked
        with a rickle of rubble
Old ballads and bones
        piled high
        in one heap of trouble.
To Babylon's walls
        I walk
        in my pea-packed sandals.
Going through to the end
        seems hardly
        worth the candle.
A sabre you need
        and a great big blubbery glove

To cut your way through the undergrowth
To cut your way through the undergrowth of love.

Lost Love Blues

The island that answered our call lies under the waves.
The stubble is bare where once were fulsome sheaves.
Now pride tries building his ineffectual rampart.

Great death is free with his non-committal comfort.
He sits in the skull and plays his mandoline.
He plucks away at one numb and deadened string.

Epistill

(aureate style)

Peter, of Cambrigge makars all the flour,
For that to mak amend ye did nocht tarrie
I am appeasit. Sweit apothecarie
Your ounce of civet is ane richt guid cure.

Remissioun to auld Emmanuel's tour,
My saulis croun, all luvingly I carrie;
And glaid acceptance - though my thanks be puir,
And I maun be mine ain bauld emissarie.

Sitzkrieg Fantasy

(A Gallimaufry)

MacSporran laments his filibeg;
       nightly
       He makes his moan:
Potbelly Abe pulls long pants over
       His old shin-bone.
The girls from Paree teach Jock and swaddy
       To bill and coo
But holy Lenin sings on Orion
       Till all is blue.

A whiff of grape-fruit proclaims the Lieutenant
       Has taken tea
While Corporal Crump spikes with testudo
       The stoat-skin sea.
My aunt Eulalia spurs the battalion
       To derring-do
But Holy Lenin sings on Orion
       Till all is blue.

Dancing the oka with an aspidistra
       Is Harry P.
He declares that a polony's aroma
       Is not for he
And employs with effect the dialectic
       To prove this true
But holy Lenin sings on Orion
       Till all is blue.

The Eireann censor demands that O'Casey
       Cross self and pray,
But Peadar O'Donnell's sign is a sickle
       And rosary.
Our playboy Dev consults at a seance
       Brian Boru
But Holy Lenin sings on Orion
       Till all is blue.

Scotland reveals that war in the isles is
        Most certain sure
For Hugh MacDiarmid has buried the hatchet
        - In Edwin Muir.
And Compton Mackenzie is seen to reach for
        His sgian dubh
But holy Lenin sings on Orion
        Till all is blue.

Huxley and Heard, secure in Nirvana
        Look down on dirt,
But Spender relates how Aeneas went and
        Pulled off his shirt.
Dylan is shocked, but Wystan Hugh Auden
        Just whispers "Coo!"
And holy Lenin sings on Orion
        Till all is blue.

Paul Potts requests that I dial October
        One Nine One Seven
And find from a Comrade Middleton Murray
        If earth *is* heaven.
Though Count Potocki swears by Apollo
        That he's a Jew
Our holy Lenin sings on Orion
        Till all is blue.

Old Tambi relates some scandalous stories
        concerning Joad,
Alleging he used to smother his daughter
        With coats of woad,
And then kick the gong around with the Brains Trust
        That *Godeless* crew,
But holy Lenin sings on Orion
        Till all is blue.

Frank Pitcairn suspects that Moscow gold has
       Just crossed the sea,
For Nancy Astor invites to Cliveden
       The whole C.P.
He hints that she has bitten off more now
       Than she can chew
But holy Lenin sings on Orion
       Till all is blue.

Roy Campbell, though fond of cracking up Franco
       Sure is no fool.
Some say that a flowering rifle is not
       His only tool.
The sons of Mithras have *luck*, but so have
       The sons of Lugh
And holy Lenin sings on Orion
       Till all is blue.

And Lenin had *luck* - luck, faith and reason,
       The holy three,
When he opened wide an historical door with
       History's key,
Professor Laski reads 'War and the Workers',
       Murmurs "Sez you" -
But holy Lenin sings on Orion
       Till all is blue.

Journey to a Kingdom

                      Alone and alonie
I climb Balmano Street. The haggard houses
Spew out their wizened withered aged children
On to the dirty stone. They puke and sprawl
And play, while in the fetid passage-ways
Coated with venomed slime, our hairy marys
Lick poison out from bloody blackened nails.
So howl, ye ships from Clyde!
                      Alone and alonie
I climb Balmano Street. They graze and grieve me,
The harsh and hacking accents of my people.
And yet in the early morning, by Schiehallion,
I heard their lovely tongues' wave-beating language.
Your metaphysics is not brazed to this,
Nor can your sly, cold analytic phrases
Disprove this canon – he who makes his bed
On velvet coal-dust must cut out his eyes
And impale them on a pin.
                      You think you live.
The demon crooks himself into your bones
And snaps them. So you are dead. But you in time,
Redeemer of us, will tear him from your branches
And tread him down into the fetid slime.
The spindle tocks and turns. Alone and alonie
I climb Balmano Street and climb to the Highlands.

                      The ships have sailed
Past Tomnahurich hill, where men with shoes
On dry land walked. Brigades of innocent sheep
Have put a race to rout. The glens are theirs.
Seaforth has gone. His doom that filled the Lews
Forgotten.
                  Coinneach Odhar is revenged
For his phosphorescent end. The tub's burnt out
That frizzled him up among the blazing tar.
The happy seer that saw not Leverhulme,
The Brahan Seer, with all his prophecies
Is gone. And with him gone the luckless Gael.

Duncan MacMaster

I am Duncan MacMaster
And wish to speak to you, Canon, most urgently
About most urgent matters, Canon. The tinker,
Who's to be married, do you remember, must be taught
The details of the service, Canon. He must say
With all my worldly goods I thee endow'
And *will* say woollen goods'. O Canon,
                    Canon...

Leaving Brandenburg 1939

A last word to the guardsmen
stalking *stramm* among the pines,
and to them that tread the Markish sand:
there are hands with wood
and hands with iron
that shall yet be torn
with triumph,

under the eagle.

4 September 1939

Bonjour, misère

We had twenty years – twenty years for
                    building and learning.
  Those twenty years come back no more.
An incendiary dawn is prelude to this soft morning
        First morning of the new war.

Ballad of the Twelve Stations of My Youth

(Here is the legend of the youth of Seumas
Who flunked the role some half-god cast him for;
Was born like Platen in an evil decade
And in one still more evil grew for war.)

I climb with Neil the whinny braes of Lornty,
  Or walk my lane by drumlie Ericht side.
Under Glasclune we play the death of Comyn,
  And fear, wee boys, the Auld Kirk's sin of pride.

Spring quickens. In the Shee Water I'm fishing.
  High on whaup's mountain time heaps stone on stone.
The speech and silence of Christ's world is Gaelic,
  And youth on age, the tree climbs from the bone.

We squabble through the shapeless Devon village,
  A tribe of schoolboys, bound for dens we know,
And act Tod Slaughter in the ferns of Haldon
  Where cloven hoofs of Horny singed the snow.

Brighton. Last night to the flicks. And now I'm sitting
  In a dressing gown on the rumpled unmade bed.
There's a trunk in the room, and plates, and morning sunshine,
  And Mrs O'Byrne saying my mother's dead.

Cramming ourselves with fish and chips we saunter
  Myself and Paddy, down the Wandsworth Road.
'Good beds for men' the shabby chapel offers:
  Sup of salvation in the Lord's abode.

So I stroll on, and cry, and make for Clichy,
  Old gossip Clichy with your bawdy joys.
I hear the workers' speeches, and I see them
  Your pretty girls and pretty painted boys.

From Acre Lane I catch a bus to Dulwich
  And read *Le Misanthrope* (an act a day)
Then stroll next door, and say hallo to Michael
  And quiz the Hogarth in our gallery.

With Frau Popo I tour baroque museums
  And throw largesse – *mit Meisterhand gemalt* –
Then leave behind the puffy Prussian statues
  And stroll with Gies-chen through the Grunewald.

I hitch-hike north from foolish virgin Cambridge,
  And in a lorry sleep by Berwick sea
Till shivering dawn – a day more and I'm thonder,
  A wolf in Badenoch among rock and scree.

It's tarzan work till sundown in the saw-mill
  But Billy, me and Cameron slog along;
Foregather in the Balavil for our ceilidh
  And drink malt whisky, swapping song for song.

From Spain return the Clyde-red brave Brigaders.
  I clench my fist to greet the red flag furled.
Our hold has slipped – now Hitler's voice is rasping
  From small square boxes over all the world.

There's fog. I climb the cobbled streets of Oldham
  With other conscripts, and report to one
Who writes with labour, and no satisfaction
  That I've turned up. – From now, my boyhood's done.

My Way Home

A path through the black-cored moorland
Is my way home, where no voice calls my name.
Only the weasel
Running a nimble courier
Starts from my stride and flees.
Now the west knows
I have come. Now night has lowered its barrier

I can take my rest.

High Hedges

"I am hoping these hollyhocks
will grow higher before the summer is over.
Last year – can you guess how high they were?
They overtopped the thatch of the cottage."

Spruce white-walled cottage with its hollyhocks,
and its orange lilies for Ireland;
the parlour always warm, and Palm Sunday crosses
twined in the pictures of Madonna and Redeemer.

"There are still high hedges, look – rare now in England.
I am glad to live here, as we still have these hedges...
Were you out on the river since you last came to see me?
I really can't remember such a splendid summer."

"D'you know what I'll do if the planes pay us a visit?
If Hitler gives me time, I shall run down the path
and lie down in the ditch. I believe you are safe there,
you are safe in the ditch if you stay there, so they tell me."

"Look at this rug. It's from Kesh in Fermanagh.
My mother used to say it was older than the Union.

When you ride down the road, looking so grand on your horses,
I shall come to the gate and watch."

Frail old lady with eyes like a starling,
bird-like old teacher in the Cross's comfort,
who often told the Board School girls of Jesus
and are now unafraid with him as saviour.

"They change so much, they are hard to recognise.
I always try, forgetting so hurts them.
They show me their first-born, and other lovely things.
Yes, I have many children."

She speaks from a world I am helping to deforest,
Where our job is to level and to clear, for the building
of our human house on the level, in the sunlight.
We have boasted our Universe ghostless and godless.

So what? – I'll not slacken in the necessary labour
with handsaw and axe, with trowel and with mortar,
but must freely acknowledge Christ to live among gods
while that white cottage can boast its high hedges.

When We Were Children

When we were children
time ran errands for us. Later we tried
to launch our craft on it; it was a grown-up
counting ten while the children ran to hide.
Or lay isolated, a ship in a bottle,
straining in stillness
against the stone pull of an immeasurable tide.

Through wash of rubble

this Time defeats me. And the headland's spike
is crumbling stump. I turn to
a burnt-out croft behind a ragged dyke.
From time past a whisper of battle.
O child, child, hurry.
For life our mortal blow quickly we'll strike.

Seascape

Pluck the seaweed from your sopping hair
And spit the Ionian from your salty lips.
Clear the shingle from between your toes,
And do try and pull yourself together.
In shallow water, without danger,
You daudled too long, morose Dionysus.
Mocker, blubbering flotsam, be reasonable.
Sit down on the sea-spittled concrete.
Listen to me while I talk sense.

I wanted to strike out over glacid waters
Over dove-breasted doldrums to the lonely pharos;
To scare the schools of plopping porpoises
And stand tip-toe on the spires of Atlantis.
But in lazy speech with the slow tongued breakers
You lolled like kelp on the slimy sea-sand,
And sulking because the tide retreated
You counted the five arms of a starfish.
- You really are perfectly impossible.

Peccadillo

Because, because the mystery
Is all, and the apparent tangible
Trash delights us, I go
Walking with a companion alone.

The familiar horrors greet me
Among the outskirts of the trees. They saunter
With their raw bones and razor-edged whistling
Tempting my fingers to tear out my tongue.

My tongue trembles to a frivolous wooing
And flutters among images. They taunt me
With encouragement, those blackamoor eyes.
The trolls are nesting in the rowan branches.

By the bottomless loch is a summer-house
On a white egg-shell of island.
To the chunking of oars we murmur
"Ich kenn Dich nicht und liebe Dich".

Grime is grey on the floor-boards.
The smell is of a mouldering dodo.
We do it. Because, because the mystery
Is all, I beg, do not repeat this.

The Applause of Men

(after Hölderlin)

My heart is holier now, and filled with a lovelier life,
Since I have loved. Why then did you esteem me more
      When I was proud and wild,
        And free with most empty words?

Och, the mob is content with what counts in the market place,
And the god of the slave is the man who kicks him around.
      In the divine believe
      Only the gods themselves

Socrates and Alcibiades

(after Hölderlin)

Why do you always pay, holiest Socrates,
Homage to this mere boy? Is there no higher thing?
      Why do you look on him
      With love, as if on the gods?

He who has thought the most loves the fullest of life;
Highest virtue is prized by him who has looked on the world;
      And often the wisest turn
      To beauty in the end of all.

Patmos

(after Hölderlin)

And if the immortals still,
As I believe, love me,
How much more then
Must they love you; for this I know,
That the will of the eternal father
   is of account to you.
Silent his sign
In the thundering sky. And One stands under
His whole life long. For Christ lives still.
And the heroes that are his sons
Have all come, and holy writings
From him, and the deeds on earth
Explain the lightning to this day.
They run an unceasing race. But
   he is present in it. For his works
Are all known to him from before.

Too long, too long already
Is the honour of the immortals invisible.
For almost they must guide
Our fingers, and shamefully
With violence are our hearts torn from us.
For the immortals must have a sacrifice
Every one. And if ever it was grudged,
Then evil came.
We have given worship to our mother the earth,
And lately we gave worship to the sun's light
In our ignorance, but the Father rules
Over all, and he most loves
That the abiding letter
Be written down, and what is lasting
Clearly pointed to.
   Thus spake German song.

En Marche

This nicht the glamourie o the wuids is daith
this nicht the mune is breengin west wi me
though clogs o ice maun smite my clangin path.

O mune, I canna hear their raucle singin
I'm hearin nocht ava but *yuir* frore music –
the mime o *eine kleine Nachtmusik*

Yestreen our barrack cradle brawly rocked,
but wakie's bashed us wi a douche o doom.
The cairts are scattert, an' the aumrie's toom.

The cranreuch maks a snell incisive physic
– an me stravaigin ower these darklin brilliant
uplands, unsiccar o the foe I seek.

Death

(after Rainer Maria Rilke)

Death is great.
We are his people
Early or late

In the heart of life's town
                when no watch we're keeping
Death is heard weeping
Within the gate.

Goettingen Nicht

On Nikolaus Hill
the wund blaws will:
whiles it's blaffy
an' whiles it's still.
In Goettingen toun
its fechtin's dune.
Lik an auld Pharoah
it shauchles roun.

Och, gleg I'll be
whan I'm out o ye.
This was aye a fremmit
place tae me.
But tae clear out nou
whan the wund's blinfou –
by Christ in Heivin
it gars me grue.

Hirplin feet
on their weel-kent beat.
Nae livin craitur
comes doun the street.
Juist toom waas, bricht
i the lantern's licht.
By Adam's curse
it's an oorie nicht!

Picture in St Sebaldus Church, Nuremberg

There is the crowning with thorns
       and one stands under
our whole lives long

      Not like the spectators:
they were here ahead of time
most half disillusioned already
maybe trying to summon up a little blood-lust
       (here and there some genuine sadists)

        One sees them often
    they are always with us:
    trying to jump the queue
some intent on private concerns
      yawning from sheer satiety
        capering
    shooting out their lips

They are hurrying around
     seeing to their affairs
        loving
           begetting children

But with Christ one always feels:
this is something which takes much longer.

X Still = 0

There are planes in the sky, but a healthy distance away.
Every now and again I can hear the muffled humming,
and think how the searchlight's fingers stroke the sky.

I am sure that a bomb dropped then – may be others coming? –
for this frail place shook with a faint but perceptible tremor.
(Like Jericho's walls it'd fall if a bomb dropped nearer).

The song that the sirens sing makes the night go gay,
makes the fenlands bright with a bloody illumination
of blazing bomber – (in dogfight had its day).

And we've had it, and all, this poor bloody generation.
        Still,
for 'history' the verdict is easy. Poor mugs, they bought
a pig in the same old poke. X still equals nought.

Phoney War

(Western Front)

It was Christmas Day in the Workhouse
And dangerous Dan McGrew
Was fighting to save the pudding
For a lady by the name of Sue.

All was quiet on the Western Front,
The waves were beating on the shore;
So send for the life-boat at Wigan –
We've never had it from there before.

Dark Streets to Go Through

Evil lurks persistent in craters
lethal for years.
    And the white unsmudged facade
crumbles at touch.

The man said "God is dead.
Listen, for the news affects you. God is dead".

The people laughed.

The man again said "God is dead.
We have ourselves killed him,
    his blood is on *our* hands
The churches are his tomb-stones,
    dotting white the land
Under the east is his head
where the priest says his paters.
God is dead".

The people laughed.
(Shooting out their lips).

We have still dark streets to go through,
    searching with feeling fingers
for the known contours of a wall, for the familiar
grime in the cracks, for dust in the sockets of the bricks,
for places where beauty is in denial, yet are unspeakably
    dear to us,
and to trace the wrong shape of a razed stump,
no flesh but loathsome ghost.
    (This necropolis
bristles with ugly angels, poised on the dead breasts
    of children
and lusting for ever in unchallengeable possession).

But poppies in the green corn speak of tomb's supercession
and this river of our inviolable peace.

Dark streets to go through, in nights debauched of quiet;
Dark streets blazing like an *auto da fe*, till cease
Well after dawn the bombers' roar and riot,
And the city, in daylight's drawn and haggard relief
Shifts on its side to sleep for half an hour,
And then goes to work, not bothering to count the dead.
Dopes, morons, mortal cousins, fools, heroes, of heroes flower –
From my heart I say it, not minding what others said.

Yet this "terrible beauty" must not blind us; men who have lost the power
To think without anger are not a pretty sight.
Planes tilting over the quaking black ant-heap of houses
will have much to answer for
(much surely to answer for)
besides hell through a long-drawn April night.
Making our task less easy.

Still, a task we must carry through.
In spite of murderous men.
                    In the fable
God is murdered, but is born again too.

A Wife Ingenrit o the Sea

The ocean's pride a winking wanton kimmer
Whose father had no love for barley water.
Each evening to the Unicorn he'd saunter
And bash his way to ecstasy. His banter
(Och, blethers! Losh, ye're haverin', auld loon.
How could ye feel the warld a-birlin roon,
How could ye hear the starnies greet, ye fule?
Is't Venus ye've been daein' wi' yer tool?)
His banter filled the heids o' ill-schooled lassies
(The while he fingered ower their sonsie chassis)
Wi' mirligoes, wi' wild and waesome dwams....
He lauched, and belted doon his hefty drams.

Pioneer Ballad of Section Three

(Tune: *O We're Rusty Bums*)

O, I'll sing you a song, and a damn good song,
   Of the good old Section Three.
We carry the pipes, we carry the clamps,
   And put'em together, do we.
We jerrymander the bloody things up
   And we sling them into the sea.
Then covered in muck we bum on the truck
   And bugger off home to tea.

Chorus:-
O, we're rusty bums, and jolly good chums,
   We live like Royal Turks,
And when we're in luck we bum on the truck
   And pity the guy that works.

                              (repeat after each verse)

We get gobbets of meat, and veg to eat
   That taste like sweaty socks,
And when we shit we're afraid to sit
   For fear of getting the pox.
But what do we care – our woes we bear
   Like a lot of yogi saints,
And if our rations were cut by half
   There'd still be No Complaints.

At half-past six the Sergeant Major
   Is shouting `Show a Leg!'
And if you're late he's very irate
   And he puts you on the peg.
For he's a silly old man, and he don't understand
   That when you've washed your plate,
And made your bed, and said your prayers
   You're bound to be two minutes late.

Our Sergeant Major's a fearless man,
   Of women he's not afraid.
He makes you think of the missing link
   When he's shouting On Parade!
He's got a big crook to bring to book
   The black sheep in the fold,
But he's got a kind face – in the usual place –
   And also a heart of gold.

O, we like work and we don't mind
   If everyone does his share,
But none of the Corporals seem to work,
   I consider it most unfair.
They lounge all day in their elegant way
   Discussing the world at large,
And if some-one reminds 'em that 'corporals work'
   They put them on a charge.

When Sergeant Mackie took ill and he died,
   He thought he'd best go to heaven,
But he stayed in the 'Ship' till closing time
   And didn't get there till eleven.
He'd been locked out, so he turned about
   And went off home to hell,
But there they made him sign the pledge
   And wear the blue ribbon as well.

Now Buckley's not a drinking man,
   Though he certainly likes a few,
And Major Briggs occasionally swigs
   Some Chablis '92.
But it's nice to know that the beer will flow
   And the bottles cheerfully pass;
They'll never be dry in the Officers Mess
   For they've always got their Bass.

When Whittington is on the beach
   The strongest men turn pale.
If any poor fools lay down their tools
   To pounce he will not fail.
I sometimes fear that inside a year
   He'll be numbered among the slain,
For someone'll lift a 20 foot
   And he'll never rise again.

Alf Lygrove is a popular guy,
   He's got chinas near and far.
When a tart, with a leer, says 'Hullo dear',
   He murmurs 'Right-o-ta'.
He lays her low in his old chateau
   And then he proceeds to fuck –
But when he's given a waggle or two
   She says 'Your dog is stuck'.

O the Corporal is a tower of strength
   And he certainly looks the part.
Among his stews I'd get the blues
   And mightily soon lose heart.
But I'll tell you why in his savoury sty
   He works with never a care.
We'd like to know where our rations go –
   But the Corporal's got them – there!

O we're the heroes of the night
   And we let you know it, too.
There can't be a man in the Pioneers
   Who would rather fight than – woo.
But if flat-arsed boats on enormous floats
   Come over the Channel by night,
There isn't a man in this perishing lot
   Who won't be there to fight.

Now, we were not a well-trained lot
    When we came from the old Earl Mill,
But now we're the Wolves of Pevensey Bay,
    The Bulldogs of Bexhill.
We're known from Meads to Wittering
    And from Chi to Selsey Bill,
And when we've arrived in Kingdom Come
    We'll be building these bastards still.

So here's a health to a bloody fine chap
    Whom all of us know by now.
Before Dunkirk he did not shirk
    As even the Guards allow.
And it's on the cards that he'll lick the Guards
    At war or women or beer.
So give a rouse – and it's on the house –
    For the Fighting Pioneer!

Chorus:-
O we're rusty bums, and jolly good chums,
    We live like Royal Turks,
And when we're in luck we bum on the truck
    And pity the guy that works.

Soldat Bernhard Pankau

I like little Pancake.
My heart is so warm.
Though he lies like a trooper
I'll do him no harm.

Ballad of the Creeping Jesus

Boots trample the boards.
Take that moan off your face my lad
                         says the Great I Am
What's your bleeding name?
Sycophant sniggers
Drive gash of eating gall through the heart of Gormless
On a skewer of pain

And weasel-keen
The eyes of the creeping jesus
With a face as long as the rain.

Moonslime on fields.
Behind our huts the peep of a crookshank shadow
Spawn of batsbane.
Queerfellow shivers.
Like poison pools the washy eyes of the bleeders
Sneer at his brain

But they're gummed in sleep
The eyes of the creeping jesus
With a face as long as the rain.

Thumb-nail in groove
Of jagged jack-knife.
                   He kens where the bastard dosses
-Hi, what's your game?
From noo till doomsday
Ye yellow-belly, ye snivellin' pregnant nun
Ye'll creep in vain

Bemused in death
The eyes of the creeping jesus
With a face as long as the rain.

Herr von Korff's Witticism

(after Christian Morgenstern)

Korff invents a joke of type peculiar,
Joke that takes effect a long while after
All have heard it with most perfect boredom.

Then, as when a dimly glowing cinder
Flares, one chuckles deep in cosy blankets,
Smiling like a satiated suckling.

When the Teased Idiot Turns

When the teased idiot turns
And in his little eye, before so patient,
The quickened anger burns
          I think with faith
Of all the uncouth, humped, hooped, malformed,
            wry-fashioned
In the traitor's gate of death.

They to their cramped ledge cling
Death's hostages from among the living people
          And in the torments sing.
          They give me power
To hammer out verse, who am learner yet,
            time's pupil
And spurn this unheeding hour.

Unheeding, because the sky
Draws eyes into its dark, and spikes their sockets
And drowns the blindbuff cry
          In silence. Yet
The blind man twists his poppies, clasps his lockets
And splits the enfolding net.

The Salamander

(**A Dream in the Great Freeze**)

So through the hard grey rind of the world I dig
Away from cold into the flaming centre.
The ice and iron spark. O false supplanter,
I find my own, which cunningly you hid.

Hephaestus was my father. In my flesh
Smoking and whimpering, fire with livid symbols
Had burnt a path-way. Fire makes clean and humbles,
Fire is the healing finger and the lash.

Kneeling by frozen waters, my fingers numb
And nipped in the whirling winds, I scent the furnace
And tear at the snow. I sniff the reek of fire.

Fire snaps the hobbling chain, the haggling pander,
And cuts down winter, stiff in rusty harness.
From fire to fire I leap, quick Salamander.

Ballad of the Stubby Guns

Another secret weapon's here
To fill us with despair and fear.
The latest things to please the Huns
Are bulgy tanks with stubby guns.

The musulmans indifferent look
From minarets in fenced Tobruk
At havoc caused within our ranks
By stubby guns on bulgy tanks!

Old Rommel's cup of joy is full
Now Cruewell's sitting in the cool.
He loves them like so many sons,
His bulgy tanks with stubby guns.

'The time's at hand' he crows with pride
'When Cairo will be occupied
And Groppi's stuffed with squareheads – thanks
To stubby guns on bulgy tanks.

'What's more' he cries in boisterous mood,
'The petrol problem's solved for good.
They run on gyppo beer and buns,
Mein bulgy tanks mit stubby guns'.

The Nordic youth in days gone by
For Gretchen or for Max would sigh.
They now prefer the rounded flanks
Of stubby guns on bulgy tanks.

I can't be free of them, it seems,
For rudely ripping up my dreams
Come rumbling tanks of ninety tons –
Great bulgy tanks with stubby guns!

And isn't it a bloody shame
The Bosch can never play the game.
The ball is on the roof-top – thanks
To stubby guns on bulgy tanks.

Of normal tanks we knew they'd heaps,
But now our fate is sealed for keeps.
Who'll blame the swaddy if he runs
From bulgy tanks with stubby guns?

Fall of Tobruk

Tommy thinks he holds Tobruk
    Along the road comes Rommel.
Inside two shakes Tobruk is took
    And Tommy's on the bummel.

He's on the bummel to the Rhine
    Where sylphs will drive him barmy.
I think old Timoshenko's fine.
    Thank God for the Red Army.

The Ballad of Gibson Pasha

(Tune: *Solomon Levi* – more or less)

My name is Gibson Pasha. I'm a wily PMC.
You bet I know a thing or two, there are no flies on me.
A fellow who could do me down has never yet been born
For I go to bed at 4am and rise before the dawn.

Chorus
O Gibson Pasha
    Tra la la la la la la
    O Gibson pasha
    Tra la la LA la laa.

I bought a very old gamous, it died upon its feet.
I cut it up and gave it to the other blokes to eat.
I pocketed their akkers – then I quickly left the scene
For when they cough the brute up they're a most unpleasant green.

I like the Duty Officer. I put him at his ease.
He has six eggs for breakfast, cooked in any way he please.
But at dinner he's less lucky, for the food I give the fool
Is risoles made from Wally's arse and Adam's gnarly tool.

I treated Courtney Smith to Scotch, I knew he'd understand.
Between us we arranged the thing, as easy's kiss your hand.
He audited the mess accounts and gave them his okay.
Then I kicked off with family prayers by saying 'Let Us Prey'.

I come from bonny Paisley, where to gamble is a sin,
Though its sons have no objections to the bawbees rolling in.
But now I prey beside the Nile, I keep the Sabbath day
And rob all simple Musulmans the Presbyterian way.

By now I've got young King Faruk quite helpless in my net
And Nahas Pasha – keep it dark – is deeply in my debt.
When Marschall Rommel felt the wind he did not hesitate
But came and popped his Bastico for LE 28.

If ever you've been naughty (for example, thieved and raped)
You'd better pay hush money, for I've got your dossier taped.
And a warning in conclusion – if you try and queer my pitch
I'll bleed you till you're just as poor as Gibson Pasha's rich.

We Show You that Death as a Dancer

(For Captain Ian McLeod)

Death the dancer poked his skull
Into our drawing-room furtively
Before a bullet cracked the lull
And stripped jack-bare the rowan tree
Now flesh drops off from every part
And in his dance he shows his art.

The fundamental now appears,
The ultimate stockade of bone.
He'll neutralize the coward years
And all poor flesh's ills condone.
When we lie stickit in the sand
He'll dance into his promised land.

Ballad of Snow-White Sandstroke

The multiple sands on the round world's seashores
are a grain of sand in the Great Sand Sea.

By mobile columns of bone dry doom
I've been cut off from the streams of home.
I'm living here off my sagging hump
On Egypt's sand-caked wrinkled rump.

The wind skelps up the sand that flies
(The vrithy sand) in your mouth and eyes,
And malice of limestone, grated fine
Whirls dust like mad when you drink or dine.

With coloured glasses my eyes I fend
From the snowy jungfrau glare of sand,
And froth-wet words of songs I've sung
Are frizzling to death on my furnace tongue.

I scratch the itch on my arms and feet
Of the blood-rose rash and prickly heat,
And desert sores on the mind and brain
Leave you far from matey, and not quite sane.

When Yahweh saw that the sand was vile
A plague of flies he sent to the Nile.
Though old King Pharoah yelled and swore
He couldn't get rid of the flies no more.

And Rameses' sins you've got to rue;
Flies sit on your mouth, and your corned beef stew.
You may stagger through sand to get away
But they'll follow your flight like beasts of prey.

If scourged by heat I pound through drifts
Of shuddered sand that the Khasmin shifts,
The scorpions leer, and a demon knows
There are gobbets of sand between my toes.

O that is the sand, the little sand
That smacks round the brain an elastic band –
That puzzles the eyes, and twitches the lips,
And worries the sun to a mind's eclipse.

Good drams I had from a kitchen cup:
The billows of sand have gulfed them up.
A curse of sandy hell's on me
From Culbin Sands to the Great Sand Sea.

Lines to a Fool

(who called a contemplative man 'dead')

You snigger at him, a walking corpse that gropes
For 'barren leaves' on learning's desert slopes.
Yet never to art (or life) you gave your praise,
Nor risked a fall, all your efficient days.

That man with inward eyes and laggard tongue
Can sit tonight the living trees among,
While you from truth under your boards are hid
And weary me, scratching on your coffin lid.

Hospital Afternoon

In the hand projecting from the blue pyjamas
The nerves dart like a pond of minnows,
Betraying a brief agitation in the brain.
Timid deer start in the parkland spinneys.
Through our shutters the fine sand blows like rain.

The waves of heat loll lazy aggression
Against our feverish island of illness.
The bumble-buzz of an electric fan
Makes a weakly wind in a covey of coolness.
Whispering starts behind the crimson screen.

We lie out of sheets in defeatist languor.
The wardrobe mirror takes up my attention.
After lunch feelings grow fat in the heat.
My nihilist brain nods its own suspension,
On a tide of treacle drifts off towards sleep.

Back from the Island of Sulloon

(for M.C. who fared better)

The dark impetuous hussar
That kinged the track with imperious pennant,
He who was known for himself from far
(The dark impetuous hussar)
Has had a come down – he slips from the ward,
Scuffing along in home-made slippers.
He skids
And flips like a ghost in a werewolf's track;
He flattens himself in the wardrobe's shadow
And holds his breath like a Gold Coast diver
For fear nurse sees him and sends him back.

Elegies for the Dead in Cyrenaica

Part One

Alles geben Götter, die unendlichen,
Ihren Lieblingen ganz.
Alle Freuden, die unendlichen,
Alle Schmerzen, die unendlichen, ganz.

                                                  Goethe

Prologue

(for John Speirs)

Obliterating face and hands
The dumb-bell guns of violence
Show up our godhead for a sham.
Against the armour of the storm
I'll hold my human barrier,
Maintain my fragile irony.

I've walked this brazen clanging path
In flesh's brittle arrogance
To chance the simple hazard, death.
Regretting only this, my rash
Ambitious wish in verse to write
A true and valued testament.

Let my words knit what now we lack
The demon and the heritage
And fancy strapped to logic's rock.
A chastened wantonness, a bit
That sets on song a discipline,
A sensuous austerity.

First Elegy

End of a Campaign

There are many dead in the brutish desert,
    who lie uneasy
among the scrub in this landscape of half-wit
stunted ill-will. For the dead land is insatiate
and necrophilous. The sand is blowing about still.
Many who for various reasons, or because
    of mere unanswerable compulsion, came here
and fought among the clutching gravestones,
    shivered and sweated,
cried out, suffered thirst, were stoically silent, cursed
the spittering machine-guns, were homesick for Europe
and fast embedded in quicksand of Africa
    agonized and died.
And sleep now. Sleep here the sleep of the dust.

There were our own, there were the others.
Their deaths were like their lives, human and animal.
There were no gods and precious few heroes.
What they regretted when they died had nothing to do with
    race and leader, realm indivisible,
laboured Augustan speeches or vague imperial heritage.
(They saw through that guff before the axe fell.)
    Their longing turned to
the lost world glimpsed in the memory of letters:
an evening at the pictures in the friendly dark,
two knowing conspirators smiling and whispering secrets;
  or else
a family gathering in the homely kitchen
with Mum so proud of her boys in uniform:
    their thoughts trembled
between moments of estrangement, and ecstatic moments
of reconciliation: and their desire
crucified itself against the unutterable shadow of someone
whose photo was in their wallets.
Then death made his incision.

There were our own, there were the others.
Therefore, minding the great word of Glencoe's
son, that we should not disfigure ourselves
with villainy of hatred; and seeing that all
have gone down like curs into anonymous silence,
I will bear witness for I knew the others.
Seeing that littoral and interior are alike indifferent
and the birds are drawn again to our welcoming north
why should I not sing *them*, the dead, the innocent?

Second Elegy

Halfaya
(For Luigi Castigliano)

At dawn, under the concise razor-edge
of the escarpment, the laager sleeps. No petrol fires yet
blow flame for brew-up. Up on the pass a sentry
inhales his Nazionale. Horse-shoe curve of the bay
grows visible beneath him. He smokes and yawns.
Ooo-augh,
                    and the limitless
shabby lion-pelt of the desert completes and rounds
his limitless ennui.

At dawn, in the gathering impetus of day, the laager sleeps.
Some restless princes dream: first light denies them
the luxury of nothing. But others their mates more lucky
drown in the lightless grottoes. (Companionable death has leant
them his ease for a moment).
                    The dreamers remember
a departure like a migration. They recall a landscape
associated with warmth and veils and pantomime
but never focused exactly. The flopping curtain
reveals scene-shifters running with freshly painted
incongruous sets. Here childhood's prairie garden
looms like a pampa, where grown-ups stalk (gross outlaws)
on legs of tree trunk:recedes: and the strepitant jungle
dwindles to scruff of shrubs on a docile common,
all but real for a moment, then gone.

The sleepers turn

gone but still no nothing laves them.
O misery, desire, desire, tautening cords of the bedrack!
Eros, in the teeth of Yahveh and his tight-lipped sect
confound the deniers of their youth! Let war lie wounded!
Eros, grant forgiveness and release
and return – against which they erect it,
the cairn of patience. *No dear, won't be long now
keep fingers crossed, chin up, keep smiling darling
be seeing you soon.*

On the horizon fires fluff now,
further than they seem.

      Sollum and Halfaya
a while yet before we leave you in quiet
and our needle swings north.

      The sleepers toss
and turn before waking: they feel through their blankets
the cold of the malevolent bomb-thumped desert,
impartial
hostile to both.

The laager is one.
Friends and enemies, haters and lovers
both sleep and dream.

Third Elegy

Leaving the City

*Morning after. Get moving. Cheerio. Be seeing you
when this party's over. Right, driver, get weaving.*

The truck pulls out
along the corniche. We dismiss with the terseness
of a newsreel the casino and the column,
the scrofulous sellers of obscenity,
the garries, the girls and the preposterous skyline.

Leave them. And out past the stinking tanneries,
the maritime Greek cafes, the wogs and the nets
drying among seaweed. Through the periphery of the city
itching under flagrant sunshine. Faster. We are nearing
the stretch leading to the salt-lake Mareotis.
Sand now, and dust-choked fig-trees. This is the road
where convoys are ordered to act in case of ambush.
A straight run through now to the coastal sector.
One sudden thought wounds: it's a half-hour or over
since we saw the last skirt. And for a moment we regret
the women, and the harbour with a curve so perfect
it seems it was drawn with the mouseion's protractor.

Past red-rimmed eye of the salt-lake. So long then,
holy filth of the living. We are going to the familiar
filth of your negation, to rejoin the proletariat
of levelling death. Stripes are shed and ranks levelled
in death's proletariat. There the Colonel of Hussars,
the keen Sapper Subaltern with a first in economics
and the sergeant well known in international football
crouch with Jock and Jame in their holes like helots.
Distinctions become vain, and former privileges quite pointless
in that new situation. See our own and the opponents
advance, meet and merge: the commingled columns
lock, strain, disengage and join issue with the dust.

Do not regret
that we have still in history to suffer
or comrade that we are the agents
of a dialectic that can destroy us
but like a man prepared, like a brave man
bid farewell to the city, and quickly
move forward on the road leading west by the salt-lake.
Like a man for long prepared, like a brave man,
like to the man who was worthy of such a city
be glad that the case admits no other solution,
acknowledge with pride the clear imperative of action
and bid farewell to her, to Alexandria, whom you are losing.

And these, advancing from the direction of Sollum,
swaddies in tropical kit, lifted in familiar vehicles
are they mirage – ourselves out of a mirror?
No, they too, leaving the plateau of Marmarica
for the serpentine of the pass, they advancing towards us
along the coast road, are the others, the brothers
in death's proletariat, they are our victims and betrayers
advancing by the sea-shore to the same assignation.
We send them our greetings out of the mirror.

Fourth Elegy

El Adem

Sow cold wind of the desert. Embittered
reflections on discomfort and protracted absence.
Cold, and resentment stirred at this seeming
winter, most cruel reversal of seasons.
The weather clogs thought: we give way to griping
and malicious ill-turns, or instinctive actions
appearing without rhyme or reason. The landsknechte
read mail, play scat, lie mute under greatcoats.
We know that our minds are as slack and rootless
as the tent-pegs driven into cracks of limestone,
and we feel the harm of inaction's erosion.
We're uneasy, knowing ourselves to be nomads,
impermanent guests on this bleak moon-surface
of dents and ridges, craters and depressions.
Yet they make us theirs: we know it, and abhor them,
vile three in one of the heretic desert,
sand rock and sky… And the sow wind, whipping
the face of a working (or a dying) unit
who shoulders his shovel with corpse obedience.

The sons of man
grow and go down in pain: they kneel for the load
and bow like brutes, in patience accepting the burden,
the pain fort and dour… Out of shuttered Europe
not even a shriek or a howl for its doomed children
is heard through the nihilist windvoice. Tomorrow's victors
survey with grief too profound for mere lamentation
their own approaching defeat: while even the defeated
await dry-eyed their ineluctable triumph.
Cages are crammed: on guard crouch the fearful oppressors
and wait for their judgment day.
        Therefore recollecting
the ice-bound paths, and now this gap in the minefields
through which (from one side or the other) all must pass
shall I not speak and condemn?

Or must it always
seem premature: the moment always at hand,
and never arriving, to use
our rebellious anger for breaking
the vicious fetters that bind us?

Endure, endure. There is as yet no solution
and no short cut, no escape and no remedy
but our human iron.
          And this Egypt teaches us
that mankind, put to the torment, can bear
on their breast the stone tomb of immolation
for millennia. The wind. We can build our cairn.

Fifth Elegy

Highland Jebel

(for John Lorne Campbell)

> *Was ist es, das an die alten seligen Küsten mich*
> *fesselt, dass ich sie mehr liebe als mein eigenes Land?*

Hölderlin

Our eyes, fatigued by the unsearchable desert's
moron monotony, lifted to the hills.

Strong-winged
our homing memory held us
on an unerring course: soared, leaving behind it
in an instant camp, coast-line and city,
sea, imbecile wasteland and the black sierras
for a well-known house.
          It found the treeless machair,
took in bay and snub headland, circled kirkyard and valley
and described once again our love's perfect circuit
till, flying to its own,
it dashed itself against the unresponsive windows.

So we waited
and lifted our eyes to
the hills, whence comes aid.

In our ears a murmur
of wind-borne battle. Herons stalk
over the blood-stained flats. Burning byres
come to my mind. Distance blurs
motive and aim. Dark moorland bleeding
for wrong or right.
Sons of the hounds
come here and get flesh. Search, bite!

In what deep antre
of death is there refuge
from this living rock?

Beyond the gate of the pass
are a high and a low road: but neither
is the road back. No, laochain, they must lead us
to the hauteur of battle. Must array, enroll us
among listening cohorts. Where both vaunting and atonement
remain muffled for ever. The caverns will number
our momentary cries among the stounds and echoes
of this highland's millennial conflict.
Another falls for Hector.
                    Again there!

                                        Aye, in spite of
the houses lying cold, and the hatred that engendered
the vileness that you know, we'll keep our assignation
with the Grecian Gael. (And those others). Then foregather
in a gorge of the cloudy jebel
older than Agamemnon.

Travelling light, and making the most of
the early coolness, we'll come before morning
to the raw uplands, and then by evening greet you
in the wilderness of your white corries, Kythairon.

Interlude

Opening of an Offensive

(a) the waiting

Armour has foregathered, snuffling
through tourbillions of fine dust.
The crews don't speak much. They've had
last brew-up before battle. The tawny
deadland lies in a silence
not yet smashed by salvoes.
No sound reaches us
from the African constellations.
The low ridge too is quiet.
But no fear we're sleeping,
no need to remind us
that the nervous fingers of the searchlights
are nearly meeting and time is flickering
and this I think in a few minutes
while the whole power crouches for the spring.
X-20 in thirty seconds. Then begin

(b) the barrage

Let loose (rounds)
the exultant bounding hell-harrowing of sound.
Break the batteries. Confound
the damnable domination. Slake
the crashing breakers-hurled rubble of the guns.
Dithering darkness, we'll wake you! Hell's bell's
blind you. Be broken, bleed
deathshead blackness!
          The thongs of the livid
firelights lick you
          jagg'd splinters rend you
                         underground
we'll bomb you, doom you, tomb you into grave's mound

(c) the Jocks

They move forward into no man's land, a vibrant sounding
    board.
        As they advance
the guns push further murderous music.
Is this all they will hear, this raucous apocalypse?
The spheres knocking in the night of Heaven?
The drummeling of overwhelming niagara?
No! For I can hear it! Or is it?… tell
me that I can hear it! Now–listen!

        Yes, hill and shieling
sea-loch and island, hear it, the yell
of your war-pipes, scaling sound's mountains
guns thunder drowning in their soaring swell!
–The barrage gulfs them: they're gulfed in the clumbering guns,
gulfed in gloom, gloom. Dumb in the blunderbuss black–
lost–gone in the anonymous cataract of noise.
Now again! The shrill war-song: it flaunts
aggression to the sullen desert. It mounts. Its scream
tops the valkyrie, tops the colossal
        artillery.

Meaning that many
German Fascists will not be going home
meaning that many
will die, doomed in their false dream

We'll mak siccar!
Against the bashing cudgel
against the contemptuous triumphs of the big battalions
mak siccar against the monkish adepts
of total war against the oppressed oppressors
mak siccar against the leaching lies
against the worked out systems of sick perversion
mak siccar
        against the executioner
against the tyrannous myth and the real terror
mak siccar

Part Two

'Na shuidhe marbh an "Glaic a' Bhàis"
fo Dhruim Ruidhìseit,
gille òg 's a logan sìos m' a ghruaidh
's a thuar grìsionn.

Smaoinich mi air a' chòir 's an àgh.
a fhuair e bho Fhurair,
bhith tuiteam ann an raon an àir
gun éirigh tuilleadh...

Ge b'e a dheòin-san no a chàs,
a neo-chiontas no mhìorun,
cha do nochd e toileachadh 'na bhàs
fo Dhruim Ruidhìseit.

Somhairle Mac Ghill-Eathain

Sixth Elegy

Acroma

Planning and execution
recede: the preliminary inertia,
the expectation, the lull, the relaxing and the encounter's
suddenness recede, become history:
                                        thrusts, sieges and feints
that still blood maps with arrows
and left dead like refuse, these are the basis
of battle studies. And we're no better. The lying films
contain greater truth than most of our memories.

And the participants? – Staff Officers consider,
discuss and record their provisional verdicts.
These were go-getters, professional outflankers,
capable assault troops, or specialists in night warfare;

while those others had guts and lacked training, yet put up
a decent enough show at Himeimat or Munassib.
Occasionally there are doubts, dispute becomes acrimonious,
the case is not proven, judgment must be deferred.
On one point however there is unanimity: their sacrifice
though hard and heroic was on the whole "necessary"
I too have acquiesced
in this evasion: that the unlucky
or the destined must inevitably fall
and be impaled on the basalt pinnacles of darkness.

Yet how can I shame them, saying that they
have died for us: that it was expedient
a generation should die for the people?

To justify them, what byways must I follow?
Into what inaccessible sierras
of naked acceptance, where mere reason cannot live,
where love shines like a glacier. Could I ever attain it?
Neither by dope of reportage, nor by anodyne of statistics
is *their* lot made easier: laughing couples at the tea-dance
ignore their memory, the memoirs almost slight them
and the queue forming up to see Rangers play Celtic
forms up without thought to those dead. – O, to right them
what requiem can I sing in the ears of the living?

No blah about their sacrifice: rather tears or reviling
of the time that took them, than an insult so outrageous.
All barriers are down: in the criss-crossed enclosures
where most lie now assembled in their aching solitude
those others lie too – who were also the sacrificed
of history's great rains, of the destructive transitions.
This one beach where high seas have disgorged them like flotsam
reveals in its nakedness their ultimate alliance.

So the words that I have looked for, and must go on looking for,
are worlds of whole love, which can slowly gain the power
to reconcile and heal. Other words would be pointless.

Seventh Elegy

Seven Good Germans

The track running between Mekili and Tmimi was at one time a
kind of no-man's-land. British patrolling was energetic, and
there were numerous brushes with German and Italian
elements. El Eleba lies about half-way along this track.

          Of the swaddies
    who came to the desert with Rommel
there were few who had heard (or would hear) of El Eleba.
They recce'd,
       or acted as medical orderlies
or patched up their tanks in the camouflaged workshops
and never gave a thought to a place like El Eleba.

To get there, you drive into the blue, take a bearing
and head for damn-all. Then you're there. And where are you?

– Still, of some few who did cross our path at El Eleba
there are seven who bide under their standing crosses.

The first a Lieutenant.
      When the medicos passed him
for service overseas, he had jotted in a note-book
to the day and the hour   keep me steadfast   there is only
the *decision and the will*

         the rest has no importance

The second a Corporal.
      He had been in the Legion
and had got one more chance to redeem his lost honour.
What he said was
Listen here, I'm fed up with your griping–
if you want extra rations, go get'em from Tommy!
You're green, that's your trouble. Dodge the column, pass the buck
and scrounge all you can – that's our law in the Legion.

You know Tommy's got 'em. . . . He's got mineral waters,
and beer, and fresh fruit in that white crinkly paper
and God knows what all! Well, what's holding you back?
Are you windy or what?

Christ, you 'old Afrikaners'!
If you're wanting the eats, go and get 'em from Tommy!

The third had been a farm-hand in the March of Silesia
and had come to the desert as fresh fodder for machine guns.
His dates are inscribed on the files, and on the cross-piece.

The fourth was a lance-jack.

He had trusted in Adolf
while working as a chemist in the suburb of Spandau.
His loves were his 'cello, and the woman who had borne him
two daughters and a son. He had faith in the Endsieg.
THAT THE NEW REICH MAY LIVE prayed the flyleaf of his Bible.

The fifth a mechanic.

All the honour and glory,
the siege of Tobruk and the conquest of Cairo
meant as much to that Boche as the Synod of Whitby.
Being wise to all this, he had one single headache,
which was, how to get back to his sweetheart (called Ilse).
–He had said

Can't the Tommy wake up and get weaving?
if he tried, he could put our whole Corps in the bag.
May God damn this Libya and both of its palm-trees!

The sixth was a Pole

–or to you, a Volksdeutscher–
who had put off his nation to serve in the Wehrmacht.
He siegheiled, and talked of "the dirty Polacken",
and said what he'd do if let loose among Russkis.
His mates thought that, though "just a polnischer Schweinhund",
he was not a bad bloke.

On the morning concerned
he was driving a truck with mail, petrol and rations.
The M.P. on duty shouted five words of warning.
He nodded

       laughed

           revved

                and drove straight for El Eleba
not having quite got the chap's Styrian lingo.

The seventh a young swaddy.

           Riding cramped in a lorry
to death along the road which winds eastward to Halfaya
he had written three verses in appeal against his sentence
which soften for an hour the anger of Lenin.

Seven poor bastards
dead in African deadland
(tawny tousled hair under the issue blanket)
wie einst Lili
dead in African deadland

einst Lili Marlene

Eighth Elegy

Karnak

Er lächelt über die ganze Welt hinaus

Surely it is a holiday
or a day of national thanksgiving–Observe the King
as he offers up the spoils of Syria to Osiris.
No doubt he is acknowledging
the conclusion of some war to preserve civilization.

Insolence of this civilisation,
to counterfeit with such assurance the eternal!

Yes, here among the shambles of Karnak
is Vollendung unknown to the restless Greeks.
Here, not in Elis and Olympia
are edle Einfalt und stille Grösse.
They bore many children
but their triumphal barque of civilisation
was weighed down with a heavy ballast
of magnetic death.
There is the Schwerpunkt, not here,
there across the river that made it all possible
the dead were taken across death
(listen to the waves of the flowing symbol,
lisping death) were taken to temporary slumber
and were introduced with courtesy to Osiris
and the immortal macabre company

      But the envious desert
held at arm's length for millennia
had its own way at last–
      in the name of Mohammed
the nomads conquered:

      though not for the first time.
It had all happened before, as is the confounding way of history:

when the shepherd kings, Yaakeb and Yusuf,
heavy breathing with their hairy gutturals,
stood incredulously in the courts of Amun.
They looked down their noses at the phallic Min
and took up stones against impassive Osiris.
(Not of them hawk Horus, or the clerkish Thoth,
not of them the complacence on the lips of Pharaoh
not of them the capitals of lotus and papyrus).

Those who go a-whoring after death
will assuredly find it. Will be sealed in, confined
to their waste palaces. And Karnak the temple
be "stalls for the nomads".

       Puff of dust
on the blurred horizon means the imminent approach
of the solution, of subjection-deliverance.
These horsemen are merciful, they bring
the craved annihilation.
These are 'my servants, the Assyrians',
       these the necessary antithesis,
these the standard-bearers of the superb blasphemy,
felling gods, levelling cities,
death-life grappling with life-death, severing
the umbilical cord of history.
These are the trampling migrations of peoples,
the horsemen of Amr, the "barbarians" of Cavafy
and Rommel before the gates of Alexandria.

But still, in utter silence, from bas-relief and painted tomb
this civilisation asserts
its stylised timeless effrontery.
Synthesis is implicit
in Rilke's single column, (die *eine)*
denying fate, the stone mask of Vollendung.
(Deaf to tarbushed dragoman
who deep-throatedly extols it).

Yes, pinned with paint to walls, deep in stone carved, they cannot
resent the usurper. They fix and hold motionless
a protracted moment of time, a transitory eon.

The sun-boat travels through the hours of darkness
and Ra mounts heavenwards his chosen path.

What will happen during this day?
                              Will the King's Vizier
find time to be present at his public function?
Will silly girls fight among the stooks: will a sailor
be beaten for insubordination?

Is the harvest home yet: will stewards be computing
in the household office the extent of their surplus?
Will patient labourers work the shadouf?
Is fruit on the branch: and will ripe pomegranates
be shipped down to Thebes? Will rough Greeks land on
    Pharos?
Will prisoners of war drive the shaft for a tomb?

Is scaffolding up? Will the subsidized craftsmen
work diligently still on their couple of colossi,
all masters of the chisel, its calculated cutting?
Are Bedouin herds moving up from the South?

Will it be a feast-day: will the smooth priests
in bell-bottomed robes process between the sphinxes?
Detesters of the disk, possessors of the mystery,
shrewd guardians of the vested interests of Amun!
Where will the King be? Out boating for his pleasure;
while his boat shears through the Nile reeds
he aims at wild fowl with a boomerang–
Can he be sure of bringing home a bag?
                No doubt the court
will see to it, being solicitous.

In the evening he will return to Thebes, in his state
chariot, with the music of many instruments.
To his fellaheen a vision of flower strewn godhead
the scourge and the crook, under the sycamore leaves of life

                of life
                o unheeding
                the long ambiguous shadow

thrown on overweening temple
by the Other, the recurrent
the bearded
the killer in the rhythmical tragedy
the heir   the stranger

Welcome O Hussein
When you enter Karbala

Ninth Elegy

Fort Capuzzo

For there will come a day
when the Lord will say
–Close Order!

One evening, breaking a jeep journey at Capuzzo
I noticed a soldier as he entered the cemetery
and stood looking at the grave of a fallen enemy.
Then I understood the meaning of the hard word 'pietas'
(a word unfamiliar to the newsreel commentator
as well as to the pimp, the informer and the traitor).

His thought was like this.–Here's another 'Good Jerry'!
Poor mucker. Just eighteen. Must be hard-up for man-power.
Or else he volunteered, silly bastard. That's the fatal.
the–fatal–mistake. Never volunteer for nothing.
I wonder how he died? Just as well it was him, though,
and not one our chaps. . . . Yes, the only good Jerry,
as they say, is your sort, chum.
                    Cheerio, you poor bastard.
Don't be late on parade when the Lord calls 'Close Order'.
Keep waiting for the angels. Keep listening for Reveille.

Tenth Elegy

The Frontier

One must die because one knows them, die
of their smile's ineffable blossom, die
of their light hands

But dust blowing round them
has stopped up their ears
                      o for ever
not sleeping but dead

The airliner's passengers,
crossing without effort the confines
of wired-off Libya, remember
little, regret less. If they idly
inspect from their windows the ennui
of limestone desert
                –and beneath them
their skimming shadow–
                they'll be certain
they've seen it, they've seen all

(Seen all, maybe, including
the lunar qattaras, the wadis like family trees,
the frontier passes with their toyshop spirals–
seen nothing, and seen all

And the scene yields them? Nothing)

Yet that coast-line
could yield much: there were recces and sorties,
drumfire and sieges. The outposts
lay here: there ran the supply route.
Forgotten.
           By that bend of Halfaya
the convoys used to stick, raw meat for the Jabos.

And here, the bay's horseshoe:
how nobly it clanged through laconic communiques!

Still, how should this interest the airborne travellers,
being less real to them than the Trojan defence-works
and touching them as little as the Achaean strategies?
Useless to deny. The memorial's obsequious
falsehoods are irrelevant. It has little to arrest them,
survivors by accident
              that dried blood in the sangars.

So I turn aside in the benighted deadland
to perform a duty, noting an outlying
grave, or restoring a fallen cross-piece.
Remembrancer.
          And shall sing them who amnestied
escaped from the tumult to stumble across sand-dunes
and darken their waves in the sea, the deliverer.

Run, stumble and fall in their instant of agony
past burnt-out brennpunkt, along hangdog dannert.
Here gutted, or stuck through the throat like Buonconte,
or charred to grey ash, they are caught in one corral.
We fly from their scorn, but they close all the passes:
their sleep's our unrest, we lie bound in their inferno—
this alliance must be vaunted and affirmed, lest they condemn us!

Lean seedlings of lament spring like swordsmen around us;
the coronach scales white arêtes. Bitter keening
of women goes up by the solitary column.
Denounce and condemn! Either build for the living
love, patience and power to absolve these tormented,
or else choke in the folds of their black-edged vendetta!
Run, stumble and fall in our desert of failure,
impaled, unappeased. And inhabit that desert
of canyon and dream—till we carry to the living
blood, fire and red flambeaux of death's proletariat.
Take iron in your arms! At last, spanning this history's
apollyon chasm, proclaim them the reconciled.

Heroic Song for the Runners of Cyrene

(to Gregorio Prieto)

Without suffering and death one learns nothing.
We should not know the difference between the visions
of the intellect and the facts.
Only those ideas are acceptable that hold through
suffering and death… .
Life is that which leaps.

DENIS SAURAT:
"Death and the Dreamer".

I

The runners who would challenge
        the rough bounds of the desert
and strip for the test
        on this barbarous arena
must have sinews like hounds
        and be cunning as jerboas.

Rooting crowds'll not hail them
        in boisterous circus
nor sleek fame crown their exploit
        with triumph and obelisk.
Sun beats their path
        down the hours of blank silence:
each knows that in the end
        he'll be lucky to have respite.

Freely they'll run
        to the chosen assignation;
ineluctable role,
        and they ready to accept it!
Going with elan of pride
        to the furious onset
they'll reclaim the dead land
        for their city of Cyrene.

Sun beats their path:
        this no course measured plainly
between markers on the beach,
        no event for the novice.
The gates open: are closed.
        And the track leads them forward
hard by salt-lake and standing stone
        blind as the cyclops.

While keeping the same pace
        neither slower nor faster
but as yet out of sight
        behind plateau and escarpment
is history the doppelgänger
        running to meet them.

II

Stroke of the sun means the hour that's to lay them
is present once more on the dust-blurred horizon.
They start, and awake from their stupor of rhythm–
and think, as they catch glimpse of sea beyond watch-tower
they cannot be far from… a place they'd forgotten.

At last it is sure. o, they know that they'll never
be hesitant feet on the marches of darkness
or humped epigonoi, outliving the Fians.

No matter what hand stirs the dust, questions gently
with curious touch the grazed stones of the city
yon stroke of the sun vaunts their exploit for ever.

They quicken their pace. (And those others too.) Faster,
and livelier now than at jousts of the Toppo.
The goal is in sight. Simultaneous the onrush,
the clash close at hand, o incarnate dialectic!
The runners gain speed. As they hail their opponents
they can hear in the air the strum of loud arrows
which predestined sing to their point of intersection.
Blaze of harsh day stuns their human defiance;
steel beats their path with its pendulum brilliance.

Sun's thong is lifted. And history the other
emerges at last from the heat's trembling mirror.

III

Their ruin upon them
they've entered the lip of the burning enclosure.
Each runs to achieve, without pause or evasion
    his instant of nothing

        they look for an opening
grip, grapple, jerk, sway
and fall locking like lovers

down the thunderous cataract of day.

Cyrene, 1942–
        Carradale, Argyll, 1947.

So Long

To the war in Africa that's over – goodnight.

To thousands of assorted vehicles, in every stage of
        decomposition
        littering the desert from here to Tunis – goodnight.

To thousands of guns and armoured fighting vehicles
        brewed up, blackened and charred
        from Alamein to here, from here to Tunis – goodnight.

To thousands of crosses of every shape and pattern,
        alone or in little huddles, under which the
                unlucky bastards lie –
                        goodnight.

                Horse-shoe curve of the bay
                clean razor-edge of the escarpment,
        tonight it's the sunset only that's blooding you.

Halfaya and Sollum: I think that at long last
        we can promise you a little quiet.
So long. I hope I won't be seeing you.

To the sodding desert – you know what you
                can do with yourself.

To the African deadland – God help you –
                        and goodnight.

Ballad of the Simeto

(For the Highland Division)

I

Armament, vehicles and bodies
make heavy cargo that is checked and away
to Sicily, to Sicily
over the dark moving waters.

The batallions came back
    to Sousse and Tunis
through the barrens, and the indifferent
    squatting villages.

Red flower in the cap
    of Arab fiesta!
and five-fold domes
    on the mosque of swords!

We snuffled and coughed
    through tourbillions of dust
and were homesick and wae
    for the streams of Europe,

But the others were blind
    to our alien trouble –
they remembered the merciful,
    the Lord of daybreak.

Launches put out
    from palm-fuzzed coastline
to where landing craft lay
    in the glittering searoads.

The ships revolved
    through horizons of dusk:
then foregathered like revenants
    from the earth near fresh graves.

Och, our playboy Jocks
    cleaned machine-guns, and swore
in their pantagruelian
    language of bothies,

and they sang their unkillable
    blustering songs,
ignoring the moon's
    contemptuous malice.

All the apprehensions, all the resolves and the terrors
and all the longings are up and away
            to Sicily, to Sicily
        over the dark moving waters.

II

Take me to see the vines
    take me to see the vines of Sicily
for my eyes out of the desert
    are moths singed on a candle.

Let me watch the lighthouse
    rise out of shore-mist. Let me seek
on uplands the grey-silver
    elegy of olives.

Eating ripe blue figs
    in the lee of a dyke
I'll mind the quiet of the reef
    near the lonely cape-island

and by swerve of the pass
    climb the scooped beds of torrents:
see grey churches like keeps
    on the terraced mountains.

The frontier of the trees
    is a pathway for goats
and convenient sanctuary
  of lascive Priapus.

Over gouged out gorge
    are green pricks of the pines:
like strict alexandrines
    stand the vertical cypresses.

O, with prophetic grief
    mourn that village that clings
to the crags of the west
    a high gat-toothed eyrie

for the tension in the rocks
    before sunset will have formed
a landscape of unrest
    that anticipates terror.

A charge has been concealed
    in the sockets of these hills.
It explodes in the heat
    of July and howitzers.

We are caught in the millennial
    conflict of Sicily
Look! Bright shards of marble
    and the broken cornice.

III

On the plain of dry water-courses
    on the plain of harvest and death
the reek of cordite
    and the blazing stooks!

Like a lascar keeking
    through the green prickly pears
the livid moon kindled
    gunpowder of the dust

and whipped to white heat
    the highland battalions
that stormed, savaged and died
    across ditches called rivers.

Battle was joined
    for crossing of the Simeto;
Pain shuddered and shrieked
    through the night-long tumult.

But aloof from the rage
    of projectiles and armour
our titan dreamed on
    into brilliant morning,

and suspended from clouds
    was asleep like a bat
in the ocean of summer
    a blue leviathan.

Yes, Etna was symbol
    of the fury and agony.
His heat was smouldering
    with our human torment.

...Drink up your fill
    parched trough of the Simeto
for blood has streamed
    in too wanton libations,

and tell of the hills
    hard-mastered Dittaino
where broke with our onslaught
    the German iron.

...A bonnet on two sticks
    is tomb for the Gael.
Callum Mor, mak
    mane for Argyll.

IV

Through doon-tummelt clachans
　　platoons of scozzesi
with tongues like fir-cones
　　and eyes of hidalgos.

Panache of pipes
　　and the tasselled swagger:
doddle of drums
　　and a jig for danger!

The balconies, fountains
　　and children greet them:
the hungry, the hating
　　the weak will know them,

Who lift in their arms
　　the sloe-eyed bambini
whose laugh crosses gulfs
　　of the lapse of language.

Their dirks in the wames
　　of sniftering bonzes
the lusty Jocks
　　who desire signorine

and castrating tyrants
　　in search of vino
our drouthy billyboys
　　in tartan filibegs!

– Gay pierrot plumes
　　on the horses greet them:
guitarists and hawkers
　　and hoors will know them.

Where faro armed
　　keeps an eye on the straits
they'll strip for a swim
　　in debatable waters

then loose on Calabria
    the sons of the hounds,
to exult in red fangs
    of vicious artillery.

Ballads and bullets
    and reels to fire them!
The hangmen, the hornies,
    the deils will fear them!

Song for an Irish Red
Killed in Sicily

Comrades onward
The raging sunward
The fleeing moonward.
        Our rifles thunder
        The stars asunder
                Till the axe falls.

Down we'll tumble
The wormwood lumber
The clutterclumber.
        Their straw and wicker
        'll frisk and flicker
                Till the axe falls.

For us no moaning
No wakes and keening
No whines and screaming.
        We'll mind the heroes
        That fell before us
                Till the axe falls.

The 51st Highland Division's Farewell to Sicily

The pipie is dozie, the pipie is fey,
He winna come roon' for his vino the day.
The sky ow'r Messina is unco an' grey,
    An' a' the bricht chaulmers are eerie.

Then fare weel ye banks o' Sicily,
Fare ye weel ye valley and shaw.
There's nae Jock will mourn the kyles o' ye,
    Puir bliddy swaddies are wearie.

Fare weel, ye banks o' Sicily,
Fare ye weel, ye valley and shaw.
There's nae hame can smoor the wiles o' ye,
    Puir bliddy swaddies are wearie.

Then doon the stair and line the waterside,
Wait your turn, the ferry's awa'.
Then doon the stair and line the waterside,
    A' the bricht chaulmers are eerie.

The drummie is polisht, the drummie is braw
He cannae be seen for his webbin' ava.
He's beezed himsel' up for a photy an a'
    Tae leave wi' his Lola, his dearie.

Sae fare weel, ye dives o' Sicily
(Fare ye weel, ye shieling an' ha'),
We'll a' mind shebeens and bothies
    Whaur kind signorinas were cheerie.

Fare weel, ye banks o' Sicily
(Fare ye weel, ye shieling an' ha');
We'll a' mind shebeens and bothies
    Whaur Jock made a date wi' his dearie.

Then tune the pipes and drub the tenor drum
(Leave your kit this side o' the wa').
Then tune the pipes and drub the tenor drum
   A' the bricht chaulmers are eerie.

Tune: Farewell to the Creeks

The Ballad o Corbara

Come listen tae me
partisans o the Romagna
an' I'se tell ye the tale
o yon wuddifu callant

that connached the pride
o the ramstam tedeschi –
in his haun a Biretta
in his cap the Reid Star.

Corbara rade south
owre ford, by pineta
tae mak contack wi 'Bob'
in his Apennine eyrie

and tae gie him the gen
about black gaird detachments
that were out for a dander
frae the toun o Forlì.

Corbara rade south:
he passed bothy and fairmyaird;
he skirted the wuidlands
o heich Sassonero

and lang or the glenside
was smoort i the gloamin
he'd maistered the pass
and was clear o its broo.

Drummelin torrent
rimbombed tae the valley.
A wee clachan cooried
amang the gray olives.

An auld wife ran out
frae the bield o her hoosie:
"May God an' his mither
an' Jesus Christ sain ye

ye campioun o aa
partisans o the Romagna
i yer haun the Biretta
i yer cap the Reid Star.

Turn ye yer ways
tae the wynds o Faenza –
turn ye an' flee
tae your ain yins, Corbara.

The Jerries are ragin
thro tounland and clachan.
They've haangit puir Bob
wi his taes ower a fire."

Thunner's black tawse
cracked the still o the forenicht.
Bluid o the sun
sweeled the track o Corbara.

"And hae they killed Bob
my ain fere o the Prato?
Hae they killed him, auld Bob,
that was gleg i the tulzies!

Gif they think that I'll turn
and I'll rin frae tedeschi –
I'm tellin ye, mither,
ye ken na Corbara!

Satan himsell
can fecht for the limmers.
I'll libb an' I'll gralloch him
for Inez and Stalin."

Killin and clearin's
the wark for tedeschi
(Richt ploy for *die lustigen*
Hanoveraner!)

Rastrellamento
an' bestial brandmord.
Slauchter's fell reik
smoored the wuidlands and vineyairds.

Black Gairds an' Jerries
were rapin and burnin:
they'd made thon paese
a kirkyairdy tooroch

an' left ilka wean
i his bluid on the hearthstane
- when intil the clachan
rade gallant Corbara.

Twa shots he fired
and twa bastards were skirlin:
anither he fired
an' their Hauptmann had had it

and aince mair he fired
i the reekin piazza
and ower the brig
and awa tae the mountain.

They were gawpin dumbfoonert
for he'd left them aa staunin.
Then a skinny Feldwebel
sterted skreichin his orders

Du Faehrst nach Faenza
ich bleibe hier unten.
Ja! Wir schnappen sofort
den Banditen Corbara.

Slap intae third
the Volkswagen lurches:
out on the road
five switherin Kraeder.

Twal seconds: they've left
the paese ahint them.
A meenit: they're climbin
thro wuids o Kastanien.

God, whit a lick!
they maun aa be blinfou
tae be breengin tae hell
i sic borneheid bravado.

Swerve tae the left
(whaur the brig isnae blawn yet)
an' swerve tae the richt
(swirlin dust on Our Leddy)

… Lik bogles they zoom
roun the muckle Deil's Elbuck –
and airse ower tits
twa crash tae the valley.

Mantrap o raip
hings lose frae a boulder
Heich on the hill
the lauch o Corbara.

Dort ist er! The Jerries
fire wild at the mockin
loud lauch – and they scramble
ower branches an' bracken.

Senta! Sei matto?
A Dolmetscher wheezes.
Rendati... porco...
Widerstand... nutzlos...

Cursin and blindin
they fire at the corries –
bairns playin tig
tak mair tent o their cover!

Trippin an' staucherin
hirplin an' stummlin
they near whaur their quarry
lies mum in a fox-hole,

an' think that they hae him
their prize Sau-Itacker
– safe i the bag
a garroted Kaninchen.

… Corbara caresses
his bonnie Biretta
"Cawa nou" he whispers
"ma wee tedescacci!

Ye're slaw on your pins
ye elite o Valhalla!
I canna be waitin
aa day on your comin."

The first o the batch
is a saxfit Berliner;
aye, nou he's sae near
ye cuid mak out the gowd bits

that gleam in his mou
when he bawls out an order.
– Ae denty slug
an' he's stretched on the bruthach.

"Deckung." "Voran."
"Ist der Luemmel des Teufels?"
"Was ist mit Euch los?"
"Soll der Schweinhund entkommen?"

Karlheinz and Rolf
mak a rush for the summit.
A Yankee grenade
blaws their shanks tae Auld Hornie.

"*Schnapp ihn!*" screams Rolf
but the rest are no carin.
The fechtin *they* ken
is wi weemin an' hauflins.

Whud doun the brae
an' splishsplash thro a lochan:
lik fower drookit rats
they vamoose ower the sky-line.

Corbara walked doun
to whaur Karlheinz lay bleedin
an' he luiked on the face
o a puir moribondo:

syne he bandaged the wounds
o the ither S.S. man
an' sat on his hunkers
a whilie aside him.

"I'm thinkin" he said
"that ye'll no be sae keen
tae be sherrickin bhoyos
lik Bob an' Corbara!

But if ye're no wearit
o me and ma mainners
the ither compagni
sall shaw ye their paces.

We'll tear ye an' bluid ye
wi Sangue an' Lupo.
We'll blaw ye aa doun
wi our fierce Uragano.

Luik out for your hurdies
if Fulmine spots ye. —
And nou I'm awa so.
Guid nicht tae ye, maisters."

Corbara lauched loud
an' he spat i the lochan:
syne he lifted his heid
lik a true Romagnolo

and turned on his ways
tae the wynds o Faenza
in his haun the Biretta
in his cap the Reid Star.

Eightsome Reel

Hey for the tall
horned shadows on the wall
and the ferlies birling in the coaxing corners.
Hey for the spark
o' buckles in the dark
and flaunting o' filabegs, the night's adorners.
Banffies hustle
through the randy reel-rawl
(loupin and cavortin see our dames from hell go)
bang through the steer
they advance
to the rear
and the ankles frisking like a fiddler's elbow.

Slash o' a dirk
bleeds the guts o' the mirk
with the glenting cramassies, the greens and yellows.
Wind cracks the cheeks

o' the dudelsack's breeks
like twa damn poltergeists at work wi' the bellows.
                    –To hell with their oboes
                            and their douce violas
their flutes and their cellos and their concertinas!
Our pipes
            and our reeds
                    they supply
                            a' the needs
of our dear wee silly little signorinas.

            Slap in the pan
        from a Billy to a Dan:
O we'll pound old Musso to a weel-tanned tyke's hide.
            We'll bury soon
        yon melancholy loon
and we'll ding doon Kesselring to dee in the dyke-side.
            Plums, we'll pree them
                with the partigiani!
Thae bluid-reid billyboys, the rantin-rory!
– Ye mean
            crood o tinks
                    gie's a fresh
                            roun o drinks
An' we'll reel Auld Hornie and his gang tae glory.

Ballad of the D-Day Dodgers

(Tune: Lili Marleen. A rumour started in Italy that Lady Astor had referred to the boys of the C.M.F. as D-Day dodgers).

We're the D-Day Dodgers, out in Italy -
Always on the vino, always on the spree.
        8th Army scroungers and their tanks
        We live in Rome - among the Yanks.
We are the D-Day Dodgers, way out in Italy.

We landed at Salerno, a holiday with pay;
The Jerries brought the bands out to greet us on the way...
        Showed us the sights and gave us tea.
        We all sang songs - the beer was free,
To welcome D-Day Dodgers to sunny Italy.

Naples and Cassino were taken in our stride,
We didn't go to fight there - we went there for the ride.
        Anzio and Sangro were just names,
        We only went to look for dames –
The artful D-Day Dodgers, way out in Italy.

On the way to Florence we had a lovely time.
We ran a bus to Rimini right through the Gothic Line.
        Soon to Bologna we will go
        And after that we'll cross the Po.
We'll still be D-Day dodging, way out in Italy.

Once we heard a rumour that we were going home,
Back to dear old Blighty - never more to roam.
        Then someone said: "In France you'll fight!"
        We said: "No fear - we'll just sit tight!"
(The windy D-Day Dodgers to stay in Italy).

Dear Lady Astor, you think you know a lot,
Standing on a platform and talking tommy-rot.
        You, England's sweetheart and its pride,
        We think your mouth's too bleeding wide
That's from your D-Day Dodgers – in far off Italy.

Look around the mountains, in the mud and rain -
You'll find the scattered crosses – (there's some which have no name).
Heartbreak and toil and suffering gone,
The boys beneath them slumber on.
Those are the D-Day Dodgers who'll stay in Italy.

Ballad of the Big Nobs

There's Wavell, there's Wavell
And he contemplates his navel
But he *was* some fuckin' use
to the Eighth Ar-mee.

There's the Auk, there's the Auk
And although some bastards talk
Och, he didn't do so bad
for the Eighth Ar-mee.

There's Ritchie, there's Ritchie
And his arse is feeling itchie
For he wasn't much fuckin' use
to the Eighth Ar-mee.

There's Stalin, there's Stalin
That the worker's got a pal in,
And he *is* some fuckin' use
to the Eighth Ar-mee.

There's Winston, there's Winston
And he ought to be in Princeton
But he *is* some fuckin use
to the Eighth Ar-mee.

O we had two Hielan laddies –
Now we've got two Irish paddies.
Let's hope they're some fuckin' use
to the Eighth Ar-mee.

The Roads to Rome

The Caesars were a randy crew –
  Ye ken the story o'm.
They tauld this tale tae Goy and Jew
  That a' roads lead tae Rome.

But for a' the haverin o' the runts,
  An' the bletherin blarney o'm
Ye heard ae sang frae a' oor fronts:
There's nae road leads tae Rome.

–But noo ye'll hear the pipers play
  Afore St. Peter's Dome
And Scotland tells the world today
  That *oor* road led tae Rome.

Ballad of the Taxi Driver's Cap

(Tune: The Lincolnshire Poacher. To a refrain by Maurice James Craig)

O Hitler's a non-smoker
and Churchill smokes cigars
and they're both as keen as mustard
on imperialistic wars.
But your uncle Joe's a worker
and a very decent chap
*because a smokes a pipe and wears
a taxi-driver's cap.*

When Rommel got to Alamein
and shook the British line
the whole of Cairo beat it to
the land of Palestine.

But Moscow's never raised a yell
and never had a flap
because Joe smokes a pipe and wears
a taxi-driver's cap.

That Hitler's armies can't be beat
is just a lot of cock,
for Marshal Timoshenko's boys
are pissing through von Bock.
The Fuehrer makes the bloomers
and his Marshals take the rap;
Meanwhile Joe smokes a pipe and wears
a taxi-driver's cap.

The Fascist drive on Stalingrad
is going mighty slow.
They've got a room in Number Nine
of Slobberskaya Row.
When Fascist armies start to run
old Gobbels fills the gap.
Meanwhile Joe smokes a pipe and wears
a taxi-driver's cap!

At home those beggars publicise
the deeds of "our Ally"
whose dearest wish was once to biff
the Bolshie in the eye.
Your uncle Joe is wise to this;
he isn't such a sap
although he smokes a pipe and wears
a taxi-driver's cap!

The Blubbing Buchmanite

When Moscow sends the call at night
"Workers of the world unite!"
The lads begin to wonder when
The human race will act like men.

And Tam (from Greenock) tells us why
The bosses send us out to die.
He says: "We Scots have gone to seed –
A revolution's what we need!"

But Micah Grant (from Shotts) starts in
To tell us how to deal with Sin –
He calls on us to turn again,
And then resumes his old refrain:

> *A revolution in the mind*
>   *will be more couthie, will be more kind.*
> *A revolution in the brain*
>   *will not annoy the boss again.*

"At times" he says "the workers feel
They've had a pretty rotten deal;
But if they search their inmost hearts
They'll find that's due to Satan's arts.

I see what few have understood –
God tries the worker for his good;
Each lustful keek at Katie Brown
Will dock his wages half a crown!

So don't provoke the Mighty God
Too sore, or you will feel the rod.
The Lord destroys that fool who fights
For earthly things like worker's rights."

> *A revolution in the mind*
> *will be more couthie will be more kind.*
> *A revolution in the brain*
> *will not annoy the boss again.*

But Tam gets back his breath and cries:
"You creeping Jesus, damn your eyes!
It's canting cunts like you who sap
The worker's spirit. Shut your trap!

A revolution in the soul
Will leave the bosses' profits whole.
A revolution in the heart
Won't help the workers' cause a fart.

We cannot have too blinking few
God-awful bums the like of you!
If just once more you try to wreck
The workers' fight, I'll wring your neck."

Ballad of the Banffies

(Tune: The Gallant Forty Twa)

Ye can talk aboot your Moray loons,
  Sae handsome and sae braw;
The Royal Scottish Fusiliers,
  A scruffy lot and a'
The Cameronians frae the South,
  They sure are mighty fine,
But in the Battle of Anzio
  'Twas the Banffies held the line.

The crofters' sons o' Banffshire,
  The cooper frae the glen,
The weaver frae Strathisla,
  Aye, and shepherd frae the ben;

The fisher lads alang the coast,
  They a' made up their min'
Tae fecht an' save their country
  In Nineteen Thirty Nine.

Von Arnim knew that he was beat
  When he capitulated.
The mistake he made was the Banffies
  Whom he underestimated.
They chased them frae the Atlas hills
  And threw them in the sea;
Then across tae Pantellaria,
  Some mair territory to free.

Then Alex said: "Oor troops maun land
  A few miles Sooth o' Rome;
The Banffies are my strongest point,
  They sure can send it home."
They landed up at Anzio
  In January Forty Four
And havena captured Rome yet
  But are knockin' at the door.

Ye can talk aboot your Scots Guards
  Sae handsome and sae strong,
But unlike oor wee Banffies
  They canna haud on for long.
In years to come, when Italy
  Is free, an' the Balkans too
Your bairns will read in history
  How the Banffies pulled us through.

Envoi

Where'er ye be, by land or sea
  Or hirplin' in the road
If ye can meet a Banff, ye'll find
  He sure can bum his load.

Requiem for the Men the Nazis Murdered

(after Fuernberg)

The hour of the dead is coming,
The dead, they don't stay dumb.

Fetters and rope won't choke the song
That wakens our dead. They'll not sleep long.
We dead condemn you. the voices drum!
The dead are speaking! They don't stay dumb.
You carted them off to their graves by night.
But *we* were watching. We heard all right.
We saw the wounds on the corpses plain
And you can trust us! *They'll rise again.*
Him with the broken limbs! Him with the smashed in face!
On judgement day they'll rise from their resting place.

- - - -

Before us still the unstruck blow.
The dead who have not ceased from hating
Are watching us, and mutely waiting.
Over them the flag we throw.

For when their eyes were shut for ever
That was the last thing that they saw.
They could not reach (by history's law)
The desired land across the river.

And yet they saw that promised place.
The flag was peace in thick of battle.
In dying passion, in death-rattle
A smile made whole the breaking face.

- - - -

O when our dead awaken
  That you condemned to death
The cause that seemed forsaken
  Will breathe their living breath.

Then you who gave the order
  You who at once obeyed
Will reach no friendly border
  The reckoning will be paid.

The hour of the dead is coming
  The dead they don't stay dumb.
They hear the deathshead drumming
  And drown in blood the drum.

When weals from Dachau beaters
  Begin to bleed again
Your jackboots, daggers, fetters
  And whips won't save you then.

And you who sowed the horror
  And made the earth unclean
Will sweat your blood in terror.
  The sickle's edge is keen.

The reaping starts tomorrow
  The sowers cut down like weed
The sowers who in the furrow
  Once sowed the bloody seed.

The crop of death we'll level
  The field of harvest bleeds!
The sickle shears from evil
  With one quick shave its heads.

The hangman and the flayer
  The flogger and the slave
For them we'll say no prayer
  For them we'll dig no grave.

If all lay swollen rotten
  Black on the German plain
The pure sky they've forgotten
  Its tears of joy would rain.

Never was harvest richer!
  The stubbled fields are red!
Death has cut down his creature
  The earth drinks where it bled.

So for victory the forbidden
  Red flags of love we'll raise.
The hour of the dead was hidden
  Now hail the living days!

Though once from mutilated
  Fingers the weapon fell –
The lust of the dead is sated
  The killers hurled to hell.

My Poems

(*after Fuernberg's* Meine Verse)

You, my poems, were not created
Like beautiful flowers in expensive vases
To charm cultivated men of leisure.
You, my poems, were not created
To be like blown soap bubbles,
Coloured glistening lies against life.
You, my poems, are my weapons!

You, my poems, were not created
To pander to gentle nostalgias,
Poetic play-acting, languishing mummery.
You my, poems, were not created
To help humanity escape from the jaws
Of the famished wolves of their misery.
You, my poems, are my weapons!

When I still let the rooms ring with you
In my homeland, in the Sudeten,
My comrades, the workers heard.
By you they were thrilled to rebellion
And they seized you like rifles
And you became their battle song.

I still see the broad rooms before me…
The lights blurred blue with tobacco smoke
Over the sea of loved faces – how
It seemed to surge hot towards me! –
And I was your brother, the poet,
And, comrades, you were my brothers too.

O those that call themselves pure poets
If only they knew how impoverished they are!
They fumble through life solitary and blind
Because their eyes can't see its face
And so they go squealing and whining
And piping their rhymes into the wind.

God, for squealing and for whining
I've never yet had time in my life.
And these days there's less time than ever
Now the gangsters are looting and burning.
My gun is ready for action. I'll use it
Against those we know of. And you, my poems,
Are my weapons dedicated to that.

From The Serbian Spring 1941

(for Marko Ristic)
(*after Fuernberg*)

The sun was cold still
but already it was melting snow.
Earliest green of spring
was frozen in the brushwood: silver grey
of sky floated over the avenue
like a cupola canopy. The rain came
and there came the spring wind.
The trees set up
a snapping and creaking. The wind sprang at their throats and let them
loose from their rigor, tore the dead matter from them
like a dry scab: and drove
the idol of winter off before his swinging
whip with whistle and yell.
He ripped
the cloth of cloud to rags: the swaddled sky
was suddenly bright and blue.
He drove the snow from Goc, drove it down dale,
the sleeping brook became a wild spring flood
and roared and raged, in riot with swollen head
high as the embankment – despising its narrow bed.

Silent and frightened we walked on, you pushing
the pram in front of us. Our hearts beat dull
and heavy through this real-seeming spring
which was no spring, for all the tender glistening
green of the grass, green of the bush and tree.
He'd walked abroad in the land. This Serbia
was wet with Satan's spittle…

His gentlemen were travelling to Berlin,
treason in bags, death in portfolios. Glossy
on special train a royal coat of arms.
The hangman's noose was waiting to receive them.

Silent and frightened we walked on. Our eyes
were fixed on the hills. It seemed as though already
we saw the slow-winged messengers of death
hovering over them. Yes. Yes. It was spring
and sunshine.

That season spring was singing all his measures.
That season death in special train was skimming
along the railroad lines towards Berlin.

Our child was laughing in the pram
and playing at hide and seek with the sunshine.
The spring wind was blowing a bloom
into his little cheeks from its lusty
lungs. How fine you travel
when you're pushed by mother-power!
                        What heavenly joggling
just from being pushed along a road!
                    And if
the spring-wind made the coloured pram-hood flap
our baby laughed!

And we – today were saddened by his laughter.
We couldn't laugh, although we wanted to.
For it was spring and it was spring with terror,
and troubled all the trees in the avenue.

Lament for the Son

(after Corrado Govoni)

He was the most beautiful son on earth,
braver than a hero of antiquity,
gentler than an angel of God:
tall and dark, his hair like a forest,
or like that intoxicating canopy
which spreads over the Po valley;
and you, without pity for me, killed him
– there, in a cave of dull-red sandstone.

He was the whole treasure
of war, of sanctuary and of crown,
of my accepted human poverty,
of my discounted poetry –
You, once his hiding-place was discovered
(after which no angel could sleep) –
You, with your thieving hands
that were strangers to no sacrilege,
you carried him away at the run
into the darkness
to destroy him without being seen –
before I had time to cry out:
'Stop!
'Put him down!
'*That is my son!*'

He was my new son, he was the triumph
of my betrayed boyhood;
and you changed him, in front of my praying hands
into a heap of worms and ashes.
    Mutilated, hurt, blinded,
only I know the tragic weight I am carrying.
I am the living cross of my dead son.

And that tremendous and precious weight
of such great suffering, of such unbearable glory
becomes daily harder and more heavy;
it breaks my skin,
it fractures every joint,
it tears my soul:
and yet I shall have to carry it
as my sole good –
as long as I have one beat
of love in my old veins for him.
I shall carry him, sinking on to my knees, if I have to,
until the day of my own burial.
Only then will we be down there together,
a perfect and obscure cross.

Poem for Silvano

Here I have wandered off the raw
And rutty track of history.
This garden flouts the arid law,
Tropic and arctic irony
        The panther's avid paw.

And all that I expected here
Is rather subtly re-arranged.
The shapes are not what they appear
The scene directions have been changed.
        Still this instinctive fear!

It's odd. Why should I want to call
(This pathway never seems to end)
And on the level fear to fall?
I think there's something round the bend …
        I don't like this at all.

Anzio April

Headlines at home. The gangrel season varies,
And Spring has gained a beach-head with our blood.
I've half a mind to kiss the blooming Jerries
And then just beat it while the going's good.
I'll bed down where deserters live on berries …
I'll play at possum in yon cork-oak wood …
    Machine-guns prate, but dannert flowers, this Spring.
    Over the grave all creatures dance and sing.

Phil shows the latest snap of his bambino.
The new mail's brought a great big box of tricks
For Donny, lucky bastard, – but for me no
Reminders: not a sausage – naethin – nix!
We hear of "heavy fighting by Cassino"
But still no sign of jeeps on Highway Six …
    In Rome the fascists lie between soft sheets
    And numskull death his little tabor beats.

The watching Jerries sight a convoy's funnels:
It's coming into range now, Anzio-bound.
Their railway gun emerges from a tunnel's
Commodious depth, and plonks a single round
A hundred yards beyond one mucker's gunwales.
I bet they'd feel much safer underground!
    This fight one's better off inside the ring.
    Over the grave all creatures dance and sing.

Last night we got a bash from Fritz's "arty"
And then his mucking jabos gave us hell.
Our mediums up and joined the mucking party.
At last our mucking planes appeared as well.
Now thirteen Jocks are dead as Bonaparty.
(Yon Heinie in the tank's begun to smell).
    Lilac in bloom: the cold's White Guard retreats
    And numskull death his little tabor beats.

Kenny's bomb-happy: I'm a ruddy poet.
By Christ, my case is worse and that's a fact.
Maybe I'm nuts. Maybe I'll start to show it.
Sometimes I think that all the rest are cracked.
They're on the spot, and hell they hardly know it
… Or so you'd think, the damfool way they act.
    Spud's writing home, and Eddie thinks he's Bing.
    Over the grave all creatures dance and sing.

Snap out of that. Brigades of battered swaddies
Have got to stay and shoot – or lose their pants;
While strange to say our Jocks (the muckle cuddies)
Have still an inclination to advance.
Down Dead-end Road, and west among the wadis
They'll pipe and make the Jerries do the dance.
    Next month the race. Today we run the heats,
    And numskull death his little tabor beats.

Red Neil, whom last I saw at lifting tatties
Pulls-through his rifle, whistles *Tulach Gorm.*
… Two drops of rain. We know whose warning *that* is.
A plum-hued cloud presents in proper form
(The old court-holy-water diplomat) his
Most courteous declaration of the storm.
    The dance is on. Strike up a Highland fling!
    Over the grave all creatures dance and sing
    (And numskull death his little tabor beats).

Written at a Conference

Show me the way to
the company I wish for
of saints and drunkards
of madmen and angels.
And the quickest way out of
this synod of sane men,
luthers and cromwells
and next door strangers.

Now a curt monosyllable
curse of derision
for bosses and bonzes
and holy delilahs.
Please send to my cell
twelve motherly harlots
and a weak sodomitical
man of perception.

Dialogue of the Angel and the Dead Boy

(after Corrado Govoni)

(To my poor Aladino, barbarously put to death by Nazi-fascists 24th March, 1944.)

The Angel.

Let us go, come! Fly! Remain motionless!
It is early, it is late, it is the hour.
Not yet, and now for ever.
All alone with you; you alone with me!

The Dead Boy.

Help me then
in the first drunken paces
of my poor stiffened limbs
because I am like a blind man.
You must tell me where there are hedges and rocks,
bridges and fords, ascents and abysses:
you do not know what a weight I am carrying
of senses not yet burnt out to ashes.

The Angel.

Follow me, hurry, don't be frightened!
There are no longer the obstacles you imagine.
Don't you hear my voice - don't you see me?

The Dead Boy.

How can I comprehend you, angel,
like this, all of a sudden, when the warmth
still flowers redly in the garden of my severed
veins, and such sweet fetters
still bind me closely to my senses?
I am too confused and absorbed
in my sleep of dead childhood,
and the insistent rumour of being
has not stopped yet: it is still filling
my brain with syllables and visions:
there are "mother" and "son" .... and "brother" ....

After the avalanche of onrushing blood that was opened
in my neck by a thunderbolt of murder ....
In my clairvoyant blindness
is it you then, new angel,
who are this breath of light
I find here on my first steps of darkness?

The Angel

In the black kingdom
of sun, ice and the dead, with one single
face, these syllables, country, mother and brother
have no longer any meaning:
one with
the rapt cloud,
and the fixed tree.
If life on earth was no more than
a tiring and troublesome learning
to say "flower" and "tree", to say "son" and "mother"
there will be no more here than an easy
and a quick forgetting.
Only then will you comprehend me
in my form of perfect angel.

The Dead Boy

The crown of glass of my mother
and no longer the thin cord of torment
binds over my breast the little bones
of hacked-off hands.
You tell me to walk forward quickly
and me not knowing how to fumble in this dark!
How can I if my head is still ....
you know, angel, how it exploded
and was full of the detonation of the mine
which at one blow brought down on me in ruin
the whole weight of blood
of the Ardeatine caves, the shambles?

The Angel.

Mother, blood, birthplace,
laborious words
soaked in sunlight

that you learnt slowly on the earth –
they have no longer any sense here.

It is as if someone among the living should say
cemetery of the wind.
Less than nothing, of that nothing
(floating mildews, proliferations
of will o' the wisps) which for your human
was the stellar silence above them.

The Dead Boy.

But to abandon like this for always
the sweet memory of life, with its sweet
pain .... to be deaf even to the sweet dreams
for always, and to those sweet
voices of the earth ....
sweet life, sweet earthly ....

The Angel

Did you think that *that* was paradise
where even the pure coruscating fire
must leave its ugly ashes?
Where the more the bright flower of the legend
glows, dreams and is fragrant, the more hateful
and foul is its tiny canker?
Are you still regretting that life of men, condemned
to wander about like prisoners in a compound
between the earth and the rain: with their weary
mask, with the shafts of sun, moon and starlight?

And your own life, made up
of inert and deluded yesterdays
which was form and almost the patient
suffering of mnemonic coral
of which the dead and submerged tree is
the entire future?

The Dead Boy.

– Help me, angel, do you not see
how inexpert I am at dying?
No-one had given me any warning
to prepare myself for learning this eternal
death, which was always
a word in my head without face or echo,

I thought of it only as a free-moving shadow,
in flight from men like a shame or scandal
or kept quiet like some tremendous guilt
already expired at birth's climax.

The Angel.

Do not fear! Fly! Walk forward!
And remain motionless for ever.
Soon you will learn me,
when seeing without eyes will turn into
a vaster seeing
and your stone deafness will be infinite hearing.
You will know very soon
what sweet labour it is to learn
the illiterate language of silence.

The Dead Boy.

I feel a light around me, and a heat
still moist and human
which persists and will not leave go of me.
It brushes against my cheek like a kiss
and it fills my hand with sunlight;
it is she, carrying her poor candle of suffering,
it is my dear mother: she searching for me, and groping
through the frozen darkness.
I will come with you then, my angel,
but if you do not want me to linger
let me cry out once more, so loudly
that the whole earth will hear it, the sweetest
name: mother
which on earth is all – is country, love, Jesus.

The Angel.

You know that I cannot weep any more .... come!

The Dead Boy.

Blind, deaf and unknown angel
why do you answer no longer?
Now at last I feel and know, I cold and in darkness,
that you have already entered into me for ever:
indifferent angel of emptiness,
angel nothing but wall.

Hate Poem

I hate him. Shuffling round the room,
A faded bloodless vampire bat
Feeding on worms in a dry tomb.
Most genteel harbinger of doom,
A withered hook-nosed diplomat.

Easy to see that he knows all
The right people - that in Berlin
Or Rome he's only got to call
And whisper three words in the hall
For every door to bow him in.

The world was all right in his day
- All right for him - but now the sky
Is overcast, the sky is grey
And working men 'get much more pay',
'Do much less work'.   (A Tartuffe sigh.)

He'd call himself a realist,
By which he means the status quo
Is real and hard inside his fist.
And sickly conscience won't be missed
If, indisposed, he has to go.

I think he once was Thyssen's guest,
Talked 'cordially' with Ribbentrop;
By Karinhall was much impressed
And with the bonzes had the best –
Yes, Uncle Hermann was the top.

The legionaries from Baldur's bed,
The bankers of the Holy Ghost
Would soon defeat the bloody Red.
To sots who with Horst Wessel bled
He'd pledge his gentlemanly toast.

And now? – The tale is different.
Five wars in eighty years begun
With brutal and depraved intent:
To serve the wargod's flourishment
He lams the bloody Hun!

By 18 B his heart is warmed,
The Home Guard, too, is sound, but he
Admits that he's 'a shade alarmed'
To see the workers may be armed.
It makes one nervous, certainly.

He reads that change is in the air,
Want will no more the land defile,
Masters and men the profits share.
He reads this all with thoughtful care,
Permits himself a little smile.

Mistake to underestimate
This fly beggar. The coppers' narks
Steer clear of his sort. *He's no blate.*
Unlike our boys, he's slow to hate
And unlike Bevin, knows his Marx.

But long enough he's had his fun,
This dodo of a die-hard race.
When Seumas finds a tommy-gun
He'll find, or his vile course is run
That liquidation meets his case.

This is the Exile's Trouble

This is the exile's trouble – the treachery of other grown familiar,
The inevitable erosion of early habit
And the early speech grown halting and clumsy.
And again we are reminded – when other is courteous,
Honeyed and wooing us to shame and betrayal
                       The little smile for own foibles
                       The smiling excuse for own identity
                       The excusing joke of own nationhood and name.

What are the dangers?
Boldly I number them,
Bitterly name them:
Cunning charity, calculating welcome, courtesan kindness,
All can accuse me
All have cajoled me
To kneeling denial.

But we have much to help us – knowledge and confirming friendship
Of own against other, and the protruding hostility
Of our less subtle enemies hearten, uphold us.
Example and tradition maintain our integrity,
We remember the loyal who lived before us.
All underlines our double allegiance,
Allegiance to Scotland and the Scottish people,
Allegiance to our allies in every nation,
To the working world and the waiting people
                       Who look to the pitface
                       Where you, Johnnie Miner,
                       Will hold a red candle.

To Hugh MacDiarmid

(on reading *Lucky Poet*)

Ich bin dir wohl ein Rätsel?
So tröste dich – Gott ist es mir.
                              (Kleist)

You admit acting out a superb comedy
Before the Scots burghers, that blubbing company.
Panache weel cockit, sharp sgian in stocking,
But conscious of something (your fighting tail?) lacking,
You strut and you gaelivant before them.
Powerless with your piping fancies to fire them
You spurn their blind-alley ways, their shuttered faces
And gar your muse kick high her paces.

If there were just two choices …
                              mine would be yours, MacDiarmid!

You tilt against 'Englishism': the words sleek and slick,
The smoothing fingers that add trick to trick;
The admirable refusal to be moved unduly
By the screaming pipe. The desire to speak truly
With a middle voice; the acceptance of protection;
The scorn for enthusiasm, that crude infection …

That's all very well.
                              But what about 'Scotchiness',
This awful dingy bleary blotchiness?
You list 'Anglophobia' as your recreation,
But it's Scotland that's driven you to ruination.
Why not admit it? The meanness, the rancour,
The philistine baseness, the divisive canker,
The sly Susanna's elder-ism, McGrundyish muck-raking
Are maladies of Scottish, not of English making.
 If we think all our ills come from 'ower the Border'
We'll never, but never, march ahead in 'guid order'.

I try to make sense of your tortured logomachy,
For there *is* a sense in which England's our enemy.
Though to her we seem boorish or just plain funny
She can buy the 'wee Jocks', and get value for money.
Although 'let us prey' is the text the Scots glory in
(It's the paper we'll wrap up our blood-boltered story in)
The license to roam through the world for plunder
We received on a plate from the big boss down under.

And does *that* let us out? No, not on your life, sir!
We've fought England's battles to the dreepin' knife, sir!
And after the gougings, the thumpings, the kickings,
We've never been averse to the jackal's pickings.
And, when we're gabbing, and have a drink to spout with,
'Here's tae us, wha's like us' is the toast we come out with.
I know you've been living in the isles like a hermit,
But you know bloody well this is true, MacDiarmid!

And have said it all before. So we're back where we started.
Yes, you've said it all before. And are broken-hearted?
You've shown up the shame of our idiot Burns Suppers
Which – when poetry's skint, stony broke, on its uppers –
Spend more on a night of befuddled bard-buggering
Than a poet can earn in a year's hugger-muggering.
The couthy Wee McGreegors can still goad you to fury.
You tear coloured strips off their twee tasselled toories.
And as for our brass-hats, and their anti-Red slaverings,
You've done more than most to put paid to their haverings.
So why all this other junk? Man, I don't get it.
This problem would soon lay me low – if I let it.
Amidst all the posturings, tantrums and rages,
Is there something you haven't said, in all these pages?
Is there some secret room, and you don't want to show it?
Did an unlucky break befall the Lucky Poet?

Just what *do* you stand for, MacDiarmid? I'm still not certain.
I don' wanna step behin' dat tartan curtain …

The Guillotine

(after Heinrich Heine – conversing in a dream with Emperor Frederick Barbarossa)

We chatted away. (Our echoing words
Through the musty halls resounded).
The Emperor asked about this and that
And dutifully I expounded.

>About all events since the Seven Years War
>He asked for information.
>No morsel of news had reached him here
>In his splendid isolation.

The French court gossip intrigued him much,
  So many choice items affording.
Of the Dubarry he now enquired
And I answered him according.

>"The Dubarry had a lovely life
>Just as long as her beau was reigning.
>But when they guillotined her she
>Had not one charm remaining.

King Louis the Fifteenth died in his bed
(An end decidedly better).
King Louis the Sixteenth was guillotined
With Marie Antoinette.

>The Queen was very proud and stiff
>As her royal breeding taught her.
>But poor Dubarry blubbered when
>To the guillotine they brought her."

The Emperor stopped in his tracks and said
"I don't quite catch your meaning.
I haven't heard that expression before:
  What is this – *guillotining?"*

"The guillotine" I explained to him
"is a novel apparatus
Which polishes off the upper class
   Because of their social status.

They call this machine the *guillotine*
To be after its learned inventor.
So Dr Guillotin for sure
The halls of fame will enter.

   They tie you down on a sizeable plank
   And then with address they shove you
   Between two posts: you've already observed
   A triangular blade above you.

A rope is pulled. The knife descends.
It gaily performs the task it
Has been assigned. Your head now falls
Into a wicker basket."

"Be silent, sir!" The Emperor roared,
"Not another word of your knife, sir.
Of more subversive goings on
I've never heard in my life, sir!

Their Majesties, the King and Queen!
Bound down! Upon a *plank,* sir!
Why, that's against all etiquette
And every respect for their rank, sir!

   You'll give an account for these monstrous crimes,
   Or I will know the reason.
   Your language is *lèse majesté,*
   Your very breath's high treason!"

Here's to the Maiden

(In 1331 the heads of 50 executed 'misdoaris'
decorated the castle of Eilean Donan)

When Moray rade intil Wester Ross
   tae further the rule o' law
he was 'richt blythe' tae see the heids
   that flooered sae weel that waa'.

Noo, efter Sasunn has felt the win'
   and lowsed her grup o' wer lugs
I wadnae mind providin' for show
   Juist twa-three elegant mugs.

A wheen Lavals got leid i' the guts
   or danced their wey tae the rope –
but oor Scots Quislings hae aa been spared
   tae gie us the same auld soap.

Ye'll see them shinin' the Southron's buits
   or kissin' his weel-faured seat.
They'd be mair use adornin' the waas
   o' yon tour whaur the three lochs meet.

The heids o' a score o' Vichy Scots
   Wad suit these partisan days,
And mak mair sense as an ornament
   Than dizzens o' wild MacRaes!

Tomb of Iases

(after C.P. Cavafy)

                  Androgyne mon amour

Iases lies here. In this city of cities
A boy renowned for his grace and beauty.

Scholars admired me, and also the people –
The rough and the ready.
                    To all sorts I gave pleasure.

But because the world thought me Narcissus and Hermes,
Abuses consumed me and killed me.
                              Passer-by,
If you are from Alexandria, you will not
      blame me.
You know the fury, the pace of our life here:–
What ardour there is, what extreme pleasure.

Chimaera

(after Dino Campana)

Ignorant whether your pale face
appeared to me among rocks,
or if you were
a smile from unknown distances,
your bent ivory forehead gleaming,
young sister of the Gioconda:
or whether you were
the smile of extinguished springtimes,
mythical in your paleness,
O Queen, Queen of our adolescence:
but for your unknown poem
of voluptousness and grief
marked by a line of blood
in the circle of your sinuous lips,
musical bloodless girl,
Queen of melody:
but for your virginal head
reclined, I, poet of the night,
kept vigil over the bright stars
in the oceans of the sky;
I, for your tender mystery,

I, for your silent blossoming.
Ignorant whether the pale fire
of your hair was the living
mark of your paleness,
or was a gentle vapour
drifting over my pain,
the smile of a face by night alone.
I gaze on the white rocks, the
silent sources of the winds,
and the immobility of the firmament,
and the swollen rivers that flow
  lamenting
and the shadow of human labour
  stooped over the cold hills
and again through limpid skies towards
  far-off free-coursing shadows
again
      and yet again
              I call you
                    Chimaera.

Wind on the Crescent

(after Eugenio Montale)

The great bridge did not lead to you.
I would have reached you, even at the cost of sailing
along the sewers, if at your command.
But already my energy, like the sun on the glass
of the verandas, was gradually weakening.

The man preaching on the Crescent
asked me 'Do you know where God is?'
I knew where, and told him. He shook his head.
Then he vanished in the whirlwind that caught up men and houses
And lifted them on high, on a colour of pitch.

Letting Go of a Dove

(after Eugenio Montale)

A white dove has flown from me
among stelae, under vaults where the sky nests.
Dawns and lights suspended; I have loved the sun,
the colour of honey – now I crave the dark.
I desire the broody fire, and this immobile tomb.
And I want to see your gaze downfacing it.

The John MacLean March

Hey, Mac, did ye see him as ye cam' doon by Gorgie,
Awa ower the Lammerlaw or north o' the Tay?
Yon man is comin' and the haill toon is turnin' oot:
We're a' shair he'll win back to Glasgie the day.
The jiners and hauders-on are marchin' frae Clydebank;
Come on noo and hear him, he'll be ower thrang tae bide.
Turn oot, Jock and Jimmie: leave your crans and your muckle gantries, –
Great John MacLean's comin' back tae the Clyde!
Great John MacLean's comin' back tae the Clyde!

Argyle Street and London Road's the route that we're marchin -
The lads frae the Broomielaw are here – tae a man!
Hi, Neil, whaur's your hadarums, ye big Hielan teuchter?
Get your pipes, mate, an' march at the heid o' the clan.
Hullo Pat Malone, sure I knew ye'd be here son:
The red and the green, lad, we'll wear side by side.
Gorbals is his the day, and Glasgie belongs tae him:
Ay, great John MacLean's comin' hame tae the Clyde.
Great John MacLean's comin' hame tae the Clyde!

Forward tae Glasgie Green we'll march in good order:
Wull grips his banner weel (that boy isna blate).
Ay there, man, that's Johnnie noo – that's him there, the bonnie fechter,
Lenin's his fiere, lad, an' Liebknecht's his mate.

Tak' tent when he's speakin', for they'll mind what he said here
In Glasgie, oor city – and the haill warld beside.
Och hey, lad, the scarlet's bonnie: here's tae ye, Hielan' Shony
Oor John MacLean has come home tae the Clyde!
Oor John MacLean has come hame tae the Clyde!

Aweel, noo it's feenished I'm awa back tae Springburn,
(Come hame tae your tea, John, we'll sune hae ye fed).
It's hard work the speakin': och, I'm shair he'll be tired the nicht,
I'll sleep on the flair, Mac, and gie John the bed.
The haill citie's quiet noo: it kens that he's restin'
At hame wi' his Glasgie freens, their fame and their pride!
The red will be worn, my lads, an' Scotland will march again
Noo great John MacLean has come hame tae the Clyde,
Noo great John MacLean has come hame tae the Clyde.

(Repeat 1st verse, starting very softly and working up to a crescendo).

Ballad of the Men of Knoydart

(Tune: Johnston's Motor Car)

'Twas down by the farm of Scottas,
Lord Brocket walked one day,
And he saw a sight that worried him
Far more than he could say,
For the "Seven Men of Knoydart"
Were doing what they'd planned –
They had staked their claims and were digging their drains
On Brocket's Private Land.

"You bloody Reds," Lord Brocket yelled,
"Wot's this you're doing 'ere ?
It doesn't pay as you'll find today,
To insult an English peer.
You're only Scottish half-wits,
But I'll make you understand
You Highland swine, these Hills are mine!
This is all Lord Brocket's Land.

I'll write to Arthur Woodburn, boys,
And they will let you know,
That the 'Sacred Rights of Property'
Will never be laid low
With your stakes and tapes, I'll make you traipse
From Knoydart to the Rand;
You can dig for gold till you're stiff and cold–
But not on this 'ere Land."

Then up spoke the Men of Knoydart:
"Away and shut your trap,
For threats from a Saxon brewer's boy,
We just won't give a rap.
O we are all ex-servicemen,
We fought against the Hun.
We can tell our enemies by now,
And Brocket, you are one!"

When he heard these words that noble peer
Turned purple in the face.
He said, "These Scottish savages
Are Britain's black disgrace.
It may be true that I've let some few
Thousand acres go to pot,
But each one I'd give to a London spiv,
Before any Goddam Scot!

"You're a crowd of Tartan Bolshies!
But I'll soon have you licked.
I'll write to the Court of Session,
For an Interim Interdict.
I'll write to my London lawyers,
And they will understand."
"Och to Hell with your London lawyers,
We want our Highland Land."

When Brocket heard these fightin' words,
He fell down in a swoon,
But they splashed his jowl with uisge,
And he woke up mighty soon,
And he moaned, "These Dukes of Sutherland
Were right about the Scot.
If I had my way I'd start today,
And clear the whole dam lot!"

Then up spoke the men of Knoydart:
"You have no earthly right,
For this is the land of Scotland,
And not the Isle of Wight.
When Scotland's proud Fianna,
With ten thousand lads is manned,
We will show the world that Highlanders
Have a right to Scottish Land.

You may scream and yell, Lord Brocket–
You may rave and stamp and shout,
But the lamp we've lit in Knoydart
Will never now go out.
For Scotland's on the march, my boys–
We think it won't be long.
Roll on the day when The Knoydart Way
Is Scotland's battle song."

Brosnachadh

(for the partisans of peace)

Break the iron man. Forsake
The arrogant robot's rule. Take
Peace down from the wall. Make
Waste the fenced citadel.

Tell of the rebellious truth. Foretell
At street corners an awakening. Swell
The insurgent armies of knowledge.
Foregather on field and fell.

Face the imperative choice. Base
On huge rock your building. Trace
With arched bodies a new legend,
Our human house greatly to grace.

Hold to an unyielding faith. Mould
Gently the mind's unreason. Shield
From desperate illusions our children,
And guide them back to bell, flower and field.

Know how the country lies. Throw
Your shadow across valleys. Blow
A summons down from the whaup's mountain
To claw the gorging eagle low.

Above all, be quick. Love
Never outlasts its movement. Prove
That with us is no 'villainy of hatred',
and history will uphold us –
                justify and forgive.

The Cell

                I

Evening is the worst   *(Pro Memoria Antonio Gramsci)*
    years as long as hours

Night's better
    the heart's rebellious
arguing the toss

whether at a given point
    forestalling counter-measures
but allowing for come-backs

        One should have

                could have

And never wearies:
uphill and downhill
toting its cargo
question and anger
make-believe and memory
up along down along
whether 'at a given point'
    the objective situation
weighed up, found wanting

might not

would not

And never wearies
crossing and re-crossing that disputed land
sizing up the obstacles, the features,
   sly dips and hummocks
patches of good going
    impassable depressions
pits holding history's refuse

white earth

not earth

blunt contours
hummocks of the dead –
and the heart joins issue
with the betrayed betrayers:
ballocky death's eager beavers
randy panders of the hoors of night
complaisant bawds of the nothing

(and this stagey night!
all organdie and spangles
the sickly moon malingering)

what was it Pound wrote

Moon my pin-up

Think and think long
mouths full of blood
limbs full of weals
eyes full of excrement

And never wearies
uphill and downhill
toting its cargo
question and anger

make-believe and memory
up along   down along

And never wearies
till dawn, noon and evening
bring years as long as hours.

II   *(Pro Memoria D.S. Mirsky)*

Memories of the undone
        on narrow shoulders lean from their atrocious weight

history's refuse, mass graves, the murdered

        corpse obedience
            filing past
              (saluting even!)
                mattocks at the port

        Our own, the others,

And never wearies
    up along down along
the objective situation
    doom of the dialectic
weighed up and found wanting …

Think, and think long
        on all that horror, history's saturnalia:
the tortuous power-webs,
                    the boxes, the alcoves,
the souped-up ideologies,
                    the lying memoranda,
the body count,
                    the tenders for crematoria,
the wire, the ramp,
                    the unspeakable experiments

White earth   not earth

Evening
          the fall
                    and despair gathers
like a stain on the white loin of the wall.

Colour of Rain and Iron

(after Salvatore Quasimodo)

You said: death, silence, solitude;
and like love, life. Being the words
of our provisory images.
A soft wind rose gently every morning,
and time the colour of rain and iron
passed over the stones,
and over us, the damned, and our low murmurous babble.
The truth is still far away.

And tell me, man split asunder on the cross,
and you whose hands are thick with blood,
how shall I answer those who ask?
Now, now: before another silence
invades our eyes, before another wind rises
and before rust flowers again.

The Sleep of the Virgin

(after Vincenzo Cardarelli)

One evening, having crossed
the threshold of your room, with your mother,
I saw you asleep,
contrairy little virgin.
There you were, lying on your bed,
motionless, without breathing
tamed at long last.
There was nothing angelic about you sleeping
dreamless – soulless –
like a rose sleeping;
and a little colour
had left your cheeks.
Your face closed, enveloped
in a distant sleep
you were great with secret ferment –
while you slept you were rising like yeast
as once in the womb of your mother.

And, child, I witnessed
your stupendous sleep.

In un Momento

(after Dino Campana)

In a moment
The roses have faded
Their petals fallen
Because I could not forget the roses
We searched for them together
We found some roses
They were her roses they were my roses
This journey we called love
With our blood and with our tears we made the roses
That shone for a moment in the morning sun
We let them wither under the sun among the brambles
The roses that were not our roses
My roses her roses

P.S. And so we forgot the roses.

Song of the Gillie More

O horo the Gillie More
Whit's the ploy ye're on sae early?
Braw news, sae tell it rarely
O horo the Gillie More
News o' him, yon muckle callant
Whistlin' at the smiddy door.
Tak your bow, for here's your ballant
O horo the Gillie More

O horo the Gillie More
Come awa an' gie's your blether.
Here's a dram'll droon the weather
O horo the Gillie More
Sons o' birk an' pine an' rowan
– Jocks and Ivans by the score
Swappin' yarns tae cowe the gowan
O horo the Gillie More

O horo the Gillie More
Noo's the time, the haimmer's ready.
Haud the tangs – ay, haud them steady
O horo the Gillie More
Gar the iron ring, avallich!
Gar it ring frae shore tae shore.
Leith tae Kiev – Don tae Gairloch
O horo the Gillie More

O horo the Gillie More
Here's a weld'll wear for ever.
Oor grup they canna sever
O horo the Gillie More
Ane's the wish yokes us thegither–
Ane's the darg that lies afore.
You an' me: the man, the brither!
Me an' you: the Gillie More.

FINE INTERLUDE TO FOLLOW STANZA 3

D.S. AL FINE STANZA 4

Glasclune and Drumlochy

From the summit of Cnoc-mahar
  I look on the laigh …
On fat Strathmore, and its braw
  largesse of lochs;
Black Loch and White Loch, Fengus, Marlee, Clunie
  where the bolstered curlers come …

But back I turn
northward, and stand at nightfall under Glasclune,
by the canyon cleft of the shaggy shabby Lornty
(the shaggy shabby, the dowdy, duddy Lornty)
that marked the clannish confine.

There were two castles,
two battled keeps, Drumlochy and Glasclune,
that kept a bloodfeud bienly on the boil.
They sat on their airse and they girned fell gyte at ither
(I'll paisley your fitt', 'I'll brackley your inverey')
… and atween, the scrogs of the dowdy duddy Lornty.
Drumlochy's laird was a slew-eye dye-blue bloodhound
who fought, as his sires had fought, with steel (cold steel!)
and said the other mugger couldn't take it.
But Glasclune knew six of that: he was progressive,
and to be in tune with the times was all his rage.
Now, one day he went out and bought a cannon
(a quare old toy unknown to the lad next door):
with this he gave Drumlochy a thorough pasting –
dang doon his wall, gave his stately pile the shakes:
in fact, blockbust him quite.
"The moral of this," said Glasclune, with 'ill-concealed'
hidalgo satisfaction, "is that Right
– unready starter in the donnybrook stakes –
must still rise early to possess the field."

Now wae's me Glasclune
  Glasclune and Drumlochy
They bashed ither blue
  By the back side o' Knockie.

Drumlochy focht fair,
  But Glasclune the deceiver
Made free wi' a firewark
  Tae blaw up his neebor.

Then shame, black shame, ay, shame on the bluidy Blairs!
  Shame on the Blairs, an' sic wuddifu races.
They think nae sin
  when they put the boot in
In the eyes of all ceevilized *folk tae disgrace us.*

Ochone Drumlochy
  Glasclune and Drumlochy –
Twa herts on ae shiv

  An' a shitten larach.

Floret Silva Undique

Floret silva undique
The lily, the rose, the rose I lay.

Tell-tale leaves on the elm-tree bole;
Reekie's oot for a Sabbath stroll.
Tim and Eck from their pad in Sciennes –
Cowboy T-shirts and Brutus jeans;
Gobstopper Gib and Jakie Tar,
Billies oot the Victoria Bar,
And Davie Bowie plyin' his trade
The sweetest minstrel was ever laid.
Foret silva undique
The rocker, the ring and the gowans gay.
The bonniest pair ye iver seen
Play chasie on the Meedies green.
Undressed to the nines, frae tit tae toe,
The Kimmers o' Coogate are a' on show.
Ripper o' flies, lord o' the tools,
Yon mental boot boy Eros rules.

Floret silva undique
We'll hae a ball, though the Deil's to pay.
The quick and the slaw are game for a tear;
Sma'back snooves from his Greyfriars lair.
Out of the darkmans the queer coves come,
Janus guisers from bield and tomb:
Scrunchit hurdies and raw-bone heid
Junkies mell wi' the livin deid.
Get stuck in Hornie, and show's the way.
The lily, the rose, the rose I lay.

Floret silva undique
The rockin' righteous are makin' hay.
Oot from their dens, as shair's your life,
Come Knox the poxy and Mac the Knife
Major Weir o' the twa-faced faith,
And Deacon Brodie in gude braid claith.

Seely sunshine and randy mirk
Like Auld Nick's wing ow'r a pairish Kirk.
Whae's yon chattin' up Jess Mackay?
It's Bailie Burke, wi' his weet wall-eye.
The kinchin's bara, so clinch the deal:
gie her a note, son, and hae a feel.
Edina - Reekie - mon amour.
Dae't, or I'll skelp your airse, ye hoor.
The flesh is bruckle, the fiend is slee:
Susanna's elders are on the spree.
The bailie beareth the belle away.
The lily, the rose, the rose I lay.

Floret silva undique
Sweet on the air till dark of day.
Sma'back pipes and they dance a spring.
Over the grave all creatures sing.
The sun gangs doon under yon hill
Jenny and Jake are at it still.
To the greenwood must I go alas
Could you gie me a loan o' Balaam's ass?
Alano I dig you the most:
The lily I laid, the rose I lost.
Whit dae ye hear amang the broom?
Spreid your thies, lass, and gie me room.
Twa gaed tae the woods, and three cam hame
Reekie, tell me my true love's name.
Edinburgh castle, toun and tour
The gowans gay and the gilliefloor.
Luvers daffin' aneath the slae
Floret silva undique
The bonniest pair ye iver seen
Fuckin' aneath the flooer'in' gean.
Bairnies wankin' abuin the clay
Floret silva undique

Flora is queen of lusty May
The lily, the rose, the rose I lay.

The Freedom Come-All-Ye

Roch the wind in the clear day's dawin
 Blaws the cloods heelster-gowdie ow'r the bay,
But there's mair nor a roch wind blawin
 Through the great glen o' the warld the day.
It's a thocht that will gar oor rottans
 – A' they rogues that gang gallus, fresh and gay –
Tak the road, and seek ither loanins
 For their ill ploys, tae sport and play

Nae mair will the bonnie callants
 Mairch tae war when oor braggarts crousely craw,
Nor wee weans frae pit-heid and clachan
 Mourn the ships sailin' doon the Broomielaw.
Broken faimlies in lands we've herriet,
 Will curse Scotland the Brave nae mair, nae mair;
Black and white, ane til ither mairriet,
 Mak the vile barracks o' their maisters bare.

So come all ye at hame wi' Freedom,
 Never heed whit the hoodies croak for doom.
In your hoose a' the bairns o' Adam
 Can find breid, barley-bree and painted room.
When MacLean meets wi's freens in Springburn
 A' the roses and geans will turn tae bloom,
And a black boy frae yont Nyanga
 Dings the fell gallows o' the burghers doon.

THE FREEDOM COME-ALL-YE

(tune: *The Bloody Fields of Flanders*)

The Flyting o' Life and Daith

Quo life, the warld is mine.
The floo'ers and trees, they're a' my ain.
I am the day, and the sunshine
Quo life, the warld is mine.

Quo daith, the warld is mine.
Your lugs are deef, your een are blin
Your floo'ers maun dwine in my bitter win'
Quo daith, the warld is mine.

Quo life, the warld is mine.
I hae saft win's, an' healin' rain,
Aipples I hae, an' breid an' wine
Quo life, the warld is mine.

Quo daith, the warld is mine.
Whit sterts in dreid, gangs doon in pain
Bairns wintin' breid are makin' mane
Quo daith, the warld is mine.

Quo life, the warld is mine.
Your deidly wark, I ken it fine
There's maet on earth for ilka wean
Quo life, the warld is mine.

Quo daith, the warld is mine.
Your silly sheaves crine in my fire
My worm keeks in your barn and byre
Quo daith, the warld is mine.

Quo life, the warld is mine.
Dule on your een! Ae galliard hert
Can ban tae hell your blackest airt
Quo life, the warld is mine.

Quo daith, the warld is mine.
Your rantin' hert, in duddies braw,
He winna lowp my preeson wa'
Quo daith, the warld is mine.

Quo life, the warld is mine.
Though ye bigg preesons o' marble stane
Hert's luve ye cannae preeson in
Quo life, the warld is mine.

Quo daith, the warld is mine.
I hae dug a grave, I hae dug it deep,
For war an' the pest will gar ye sleep.
Quo daith, the warld is mine.

Quo life, the warld is mine.
An open grave is a furrow syne.
Ye'll no keep my seed frae fa'in in.
Quo life the warld is mine.

Jokers abounding

(for Peter Duval Smith)

Jokers abounding
who jouk the wuddy
and fly for refuge
to the horned mystery
I'll acclaim the accomplished
who wield two-edged history.

In council or ambush
adroit and graceful
or for twenty years
their barred sky scanning,
the apollyon abysses
with their bodies spanning,

they learn in due time
to take the measure
of bumpkin death
and his uncouth dalliance
Ay, brought to the ring
they'll dance a galliard.

To jouk in the leeside
of lumpen Jesus –
or walk alert
without guide or ally
through glowering ravine
and too-silent valley:

Peter, facing that journey
my wish is yours
to emerge with luck
from history's ambuscades,
and surely to encompass
the crossed sword-blades.

Auld Reekie's Roses

That hoor the dawn is rouging
The Portobello Road.
A clapper over cobbles
The lorries bum their load.

Lay the lily O
O lay the lily O

Through Jessie's wanton window
A single bulb still burns.
The tall chain-smoking chimney
Stands by while Jessie earns.

At stair and close and vennel
The grimy day keeks in.
The wayside pulpit calls us
To keep it free from sin.

Wake up, wake up Alanna
The room is full of light.
I've got to earn my loving
It can't be always night.

Alonie and alonie
You'll have to bide your lane.
There's Woodbines in the dresser
And a lolly for the wean.

He walks down by the fun-fair
A cold forsaken den.
Tarpaulin drapes the gee-gees
Til Destry rides again.

A breeze from Inchcolm swithers,
Flakes oot amang the groins.
The bells of doom come jangling
From Calvin's stony loins.

Day empty day advances:
A siren skreichs in pain.
Up vennel, close and stairheid
The wifies mak their mane.

O would you be a sodger
And list with Sergeant Death –
Queen's shillings in his sporran
And whisky on his breath.

Or would you be a charmer
Aloft where angels sing?
The monumental mason
Will clip that angel's wing.

Lay the lily O
O lay the lily O

Day empty day advances
Gives lightsome dawn the lie.
The wayside pulpit calls us
To seek our joys on high.

The brothel-banks are open –
They cater for all needs.
The fozy voyeurs gather
To watch how money breeds.

But when the fun-fair opens
And bairnies ride the range,
The Oriental Gambler
Will snitch their smallest change.

Lay the lily O
O lay the lily O

Wake up then Camerados
It's time to make a move.
You can't be aye beach-combing
On lucky shores of love.

The brothel-bank's for busting,
The inmates all set free.
The Kirk, that dour dissembler,
We'll brak its back in three.

This seely Earth's our Salem
To Hell with Kingdom Come.
If Sergeant Death struts near us,
We'll slash his painted drum.

The wayside pulpit's dredgy
Can soond for ither lugs.
The joys o' Heaven we'll leave til
The angels – and the speugs.

      Lay the lily O
      O lay the lily O

      Lay the lily O
      O lay the lily O

Rivonia

(Tune: Viva la 15 Brigata)

They have sentenced the men of Rivonia
Rumbala rumbala rumba la
The comrades of Nelson Mandela
Rumbala rumbala rumba la
He is buried alive on an island
Free Mandela Free Mandela
He is buried alive on an island
Free Mandela Free Mandela

Verwoerd feared the mind of Mandela
Rumbala rumbala rumba la
He was stifling the voice of Mandela
Rumbala rumbala rumba la
Free Mbeki Goldberg Sisulu
Free Mandela free Mandela
Free Mbeki Goldberg Sisulu
Free Mandela Free Mandela

The crime of the men of Rivonia
Rumbala rumbala rumba la
Was to organise farmer and miner
Rumbala rumbala rumba la
Against baaskap and sjambok and keerie
Free Mandela Free Mandela
Against baaskap and sjambok and keerie
Free Mandela Free Mandela

Set free the men of Rivonia
Rumbala rumbala rumba la
Break down the walls of their prison
Rumbala rumbala rumba la
Freedom and justice Uhuru
Free Mandela Free Mandela
Freedom and Justice Uhuru
Free Mandela Free Mandela

Power to the heirs of Luthuli
Rumbala rumbala rumba la
The comrades of Nelson Mandela
Rumbala rumbala rumba la
Spear of the Nation unbroken
Free Mandela Free Mandela
Amandla Umkhonto we Sizwe
Free Mandela Free Mandela

Epistle to Mary

(on receiving an invite to cross the Meedie.)

Dear Mary, ye'll hae heard the baur
A news-bound peddled near and faur
That hobnailed tramplins in the glaur

Or punch-ups bluidy
Await the hardy souls wha daur

Tae cross the Meedie!

A thowless game they skellums play
Wha manufacture scares for pay.
Guid kens the donnert things they'll say

Tae pad an article,
Although it's plain o' sense they've nae

The sma'est particle.

A hangin' Judge, by name MacQueen,
In Twenty-Eicht dwalt snod and bien.
Frae's wark he'd wander hame his leen

Nor mak it speedy!
And whiles, tae ceilidh on a freen,

He'd cross the Meedie.

What he could dae, and freely did,
When croods were yellin' for his bluid,
We honest fowk, for Scotland's guid

(And oor ane tummies)
Will shairly dae, seein' we are bid,

And pree yir yummies!

Though noddies gether in the mirk
Wi' gullie knives, tae dae a Burke;
Though a' Young Niddrie Terrors lurk

Wi' een sae beady –
For them I winna gie a firk.

I'll cross the Meedie!

We'll step it oot tae George's Square
And sample a' this "hamely fare" –
Although exotic's mebbe mair

The word I'm seekin'!
We'll pree the fleshpots, while they're there,

And never weaken.

Though in oor path the lichtnins flash,
Or Orange bowsies sing the Sash,
We'll run the risk o' bein' ca'd rash

Or just plain greedy!
Wi'oot a doot we'll hae a bash.

We'll cross the Meedie.

To Stuart – on his Leaving for Jamaica

Gae fetch tae us twa bolls o' malt,
The best that Sandy's can provide us,
And syne anither twa lay doon
As sune's we get the first inside us.
Scotch drink and sang hae aye been fieres;
Whisky and Stuart gang thegither:
Sae when the partin' gless we've drained,
We'll no' be sweir tae hae anither!

The boat that rocks aside the pier
Will rock some mair when ye are on it.
Its deck will tilt and stand up hie
Tae match the tilt o' Stuart's bonnet.
On Kingston strand the dusky dames
For sportive romps will soon prepare 'em;
Spyin' the shape o' things to come,
They'll soon resolve tae grin an' bear 'em.

Stuart, atween us braid maun roll
"A waste of seas" – a vale o' water.
(What signifies a waste o' seas?
A waste o' beer's anither maitter.)
But, in their cups, in auld Bell's bar,
The Legion o' the Damned will mind ye;
And howp that, noo and then, ye'll toast
The gallus crew ye've left behind ye.

Under the Earth I Go

Under the earth I go
On the oak-leaf I stand
I ride on the filly that never was foaled
And I carry the dead in my hand

There's method in my magic!

Seeing I have passed my sell-by date
And will no doubt be hanging up my clogs quite soon
I have come back to Padstow to dance - to dance!

Doddle of drums on a May morning
Slash of sunlight on hill and harbour
High-jacked greenwood louping along the quay

To hell with Aunt Ursula Birdhood
And her auld yowe deid in the park.
While my love lives, I'll dance with the Mayers
Teasing the Old Oss till there's new life in him
Chasing sweet lusty Spring with pipes, goatskin and bones.

Sunshowers over the estuary
Cormorant black on the pale sands yonder
Taste of dank earth on my tongue
Trembling oak-leaves coortin' the Sun,
And the twin dragons, Life and Death,
Jousting thegither under the Maypole.

Change elegy into hymn, remake it –
Don't fail again. Like the potent
Sap in these branches, once bare, and now brimming
With routh of green leavery,
remake it, and renew.

Makar, ye maun sing them –
Cantos of exploit and dream,
Dain of desire and fulfilment,
Ballants of fire and red flambeaux...

Tomorrow, songs
Will flow free again, and new voices
Be borne on the carrying stream

Asleep in Spring sunshine
Cornish riverbanks
Flower again!

Back in Fyvie's lands
I'll say fareweel wi' the plooman's week:

Soor Monday
Cauld Tysday
Cruel Wednesday
Everlasting Thursday
On Friday – will ye n'er get duin!
Sweet Setterday, and the efternuin
Glorious Sunday – rest forever.

Amen.

Notes

Bridge Street Blues: Given its premiere in the clubrooms of the Cambridge University Socialist Club in May 1939, to the jazz guitar accompaniment of Peter Paston Brown.

Epistill: Addressed to Peter Paston Brown, a close friend of mine at Cambridge. A bomber pilot in the RAFVR, he was shot down over France on June 20th 1943. He was 23.

Journey to a Kingdom: Written as part of a longer, unfinished sequence (August 1940).

4 September 1939: This quatrain was written about 6am in Kensington Gardens. I had spent the night under a tree there, having almost no money, and no place to stay in London. The previous day I had hitch-hiked from Ledbury in Herefordshire, the HQ of a Quaker organisation for which I worked from several weeks in Nazi Germany that summer. I heard of the declaration of war en route to London.

Ballad of Twelve Stations of My Youth: Graf Platen, a German poet mocked by Heine. "Where cloven hooves of Horny singed the snow" refers to a local legend of the Devon village of Haldon. "mit Meisterhand gemalt" – with a Master's hand.

High Hedges: Written at Hardwicke, Cambridge, June, 1940.

Peccadillo: "Ich kenn Dich nich und liebe Dich" – I don't know you and I love you.

Patmos: This is an extract from one of the greatest poems in the German language and one can see in its highest expression the sensitive and imaginative genius of the German people, a people whose great traditions were debauched by the abominable tyranny of Nazism.

Death: Written in Egypt not long after I arrived.

X Still = 0: Written during the air raid on Cambridge, June 13/14, 1940. Expecting my call-up papers daily, I stayed on in my Cambridge digs after the end of the summer term of 1940. I was sitting reading Cyril Connolly's *Enemies of Promise* one night in June when the warning sirens sounded and I heard the first bombs falling on Cambridge.

A rumour circulated that Baldur von Schirach, Hitler's youth leader, had said that bombs on Oxford and Cambridge would bring Britain to her knees. Oddly enough, this, and the equally preposterous rumour that Hitler had only one testicle, turned out to be true.

Pioneer Ballad of Section Three: This ballad, founded on a well-known bum song, was made up by me while I was, with my mates in the Pioneers, building the scaffolding boom defence on the beaches of south-east England. It became very popular, was sung by everyone and was (in a bowlderdized version) the hit of two concerts. The communal making of it (several of my mates contributed ideas, lines and snatches of stanzas) and the variants which it rapidly developed on the lips of others gave me valuable insight into folk poetry in action.

While in Wittering we lived in `chalets' (i.e. ramshackle holiday camp huts). Lygrove, whose Cockney speech was as vivid as Synge's Playboy, called his `The Chateau'. I called mine Rustibums.

The Earl Mill at Oldham had been our training centre and I was there for a fortnight.

Soldat Bernhard Pankau: Written during his interrogation. He was a German trooper captured in the desert. He came clean but had no high level intelligence to offer.

The Ballad of the Creeping Jesus: This poem, one of a series of grotesques, is a revenge tragedy of the Army underworld.

A' queerfellow' is betrayed by his mate, the sneak, called a 'Creeping Jesus'. The halfwit, after doing a course of punishment called 'jankers', pursues his friend with a vendetta and makes an attempt on his life with a jack-knife.

The first verse is company orders, where the queerfellow is convicted on his friend's evidence for a crime which the latter committed.

The second is the desire for vengeance, in a cold landscape of moonlight.

The third is the resolve taken, and the deed done.

Herr von Korff's Witticism: Morgenstern was a German humorous poet.

Ballad of the Stubby Guns: I wrote this on June 1942, the day before Tobruk fell.

In the hectic days of Rommel's offensive an extraordinary report was current (it emanated from the heated brain of an intelligence officer) that the Germans were using on their new tanks hollow armour of such abnormal thickness that it gave the gun mounted on the tank a "stubby" appearance.

Cruewell – a German general and rival to Rommel.

Groppi's – a Cairo restaurant.

The Ballad of Gibson Pasha: Written in 1942, Gibson Pasha is a fictitious character who acts as a symbol of the kind of predatory small mind not unknown in times of war.

We Show You that Death as a Dancer: Written at Alamein, 1942.

Ballad of Snow White Sandstroke: After the fall of Tobruk – which the previous year had remained in our hands, an unconquered fortress – on 20 June 1942, Rommel's Africa Korps invaded Egypt, and it had reached to within sixty miles of Alexandria, before it was brought to a halt by the 2nd New Zealand Division, in the first battle of Alamein. On the 13th of August Montgomery arrived in the desert to take command of the Eighth Army, and at once began to prepare for a defensive battle against the renewed German offensive which was bound to come.

Rommel's order of the day on August 30th called on his men to advance and capture Alex, Cairo and the Delta; instead he was decisively beaten by the tanks and anti-tank guns dug in on the height of Alam Halfa, and was obliged to withdraw, leaving behind 49 tanks, 55 guns, 395 vehicles and 2,910 dead.

After the enemy's retreat I was given the job of taking a jeep through the minefields and counting the still smoking and smouldering armoured fighting vehicles and guns lying around on the now empty desert battlefield; because of the uncertain distances and directions I ticked them off with a piece of chalk, in order to make sure I was not counting the same ones twice!

In his book *Panzer Battles*, von Mellenthin described Alam Halfa as "the turning point of the desert war, and the first of a long series of defeats on every front which foreshadowed the defeat of Germany".

Back from the Island of Sulloon: This and the previous poem were both written in Helwan General Hospital just south of Cairo in 1942. I was in hospital with some kind of dysentry thing. This chap was an officer in the 8th Army, in a tank regiment. He was badly damaged physically.

Notes to Elegies:

The quotations used to introduce the two parts of the cycle need, perhaps, a word of elucidation. Goethe's quatrain was frequently included in small anthologies "for the Front" carried by German soldiers in the field – and indeed its thought lies very near the mood of many of them. One might translate it as follows:

"The gods, the unending, give all things without stint to their beloved: all pleasures, the unending – and all pains, the unending, without stint".

Set against this as the beginning of the second part is the sceptical ironic spirit of a Gaelic poet who fought in the desert and was wounded at El Alamein. Sorley MacLean translates his own poem thus:

"Sitting dead in 'Death Valley' below the Ruweisat Ridge, a boy with his forelock down about his cheek and his face slate-grey. I thought of the right and joy he had from his Fuehrer, of falling in the field of slaughter to rise no more.... Whatever his desire or mishap, his innocence or malignance, he showed no pleasure in his death below the Ruweisat Ridge".

Third Elegy :   The quotations in this poem are from "The God Leaves Anthony" by the Greek Alexandrian poet, C. P. Cavafy (1868-1933).

In Cavafy's poem, Alexandria is a symbol of life itself.

Fifth Elegy : *Laochain.* Literally means "little hero". Familiar term of endearment for a young lad in Gaelic.

Another falls for Hector. Patroclus. – I was thinking also of the warcry of the Macleans who died in defence of their chief at Inverkeithing: Fear eile airson Eachainn (Another for Hector)

The Grecian Gael. Term occasionally used by the old bards for the Scots and Irish – Cf. the *Brosnachadh* (Incitement to Rise) addressed to Argyll before Flodden. (Book of the Dean of Lismore).

Interlude :

Scaling sound's mountains.
    Wi' nocht but the cry o' the pipes can Earth
    Or these – or silence – meet.
                        Hugh MacDiarmid. *Coronach for the End of the World.*

Mak siccar (Make sure). One of the famous phrases of mediaeval Scottish history.
After Bruce had stabbed the Red Comyn in Dumfries Kirk he was found outside the building by Lindsay and Kirkpatrick. Lindsay asked if Comyn were dead. Bruce replied that he didn't know. "Aweel", said Kirkpatrick, "I'll mak siccar".

Eighth Elegy : "This civilisation was filled, so great was its unshaken complacence on this earth, with a profound death-longing – it longed, dreamed, lusted, went a-whoring after death.

"Karnak, smashed, is the ironic image of Vollendung. The tombs in the Valley of the Kings are as good a sketch as man made of 'the eternal'.

"I do not let myself be weighed down by the impassive timeless effrontery of this civilisation. I realise that all of us, from Hellenes to Gaelic outlanders of the western world are in a sense beside Thebes half civilised clod-hoppers, hairy men with a lop-sided slant on time, half-baked hurried ignorant Yank tourists with a kink about progress mechanical or social.

"But you can have Luxor – it solves none of the problems, it doesn't even pose them.If we of the modern west devote a tenth of the time to life that Karnak devoted to death, we'll bring a tangible hope, even to the inhabitants of the Nile Valley".
– Extract from my notebook, 17 January 1943.

The "barbarians" of Cavafy. I was thinking of these lines in the poem "Waiting for the Barbarians":

        "And now what is to become of us without barbarians?
        These barbarians were a kind of solution".

He aims at wildfowl with a boomerang. If any one doubts the authenticity of this reference, he should pay a visit to the tomb of Menna, which is among the nobles' tombs at Thebes.

Ninth Elegy : *The newsreel commentator.* I was thinking particularly of one whose mike-side manner when referring to the area targets of Bomber Command or when delivering ignoble gibes at the expense of enemy front-line soldiers filled me (and plenty of others) with shame and fury.

Tenth Elegy : *Stuck through the throat like Buonconte.* Dante Purg. V. 88-129.
The episode of Buonconte was quoted to me by a Tuscan partisan in the hills north of Florence.

Heroic Song for the Runners of Cyrene : Cyrene in this poem is for me a symbol of civilised humanity, of our "human house". The legend of the brothers Philaeni who competed against athletes from Cyrene suggested the symbol of the runners.
History the doppelgänger.

> "Spectre of Albion! Warlike fiend!
> In clouds of blood and ruin rolled,
> I here reclaim thee as my own!
> My selfhood! Satan! Arm'd in gold."

> William Blake.

They cannot be far from. I had in my mind here a line which introduces the Skaggerrak motif in Reinhold Goering's play *Seeschlacht* (Sea Battle) – "We cannot be far from the Skaggerrak".

Seeschlacht which appeared in 1917 was inspired by the Battle of Jutland fought the previous year – a battle known in German as the Skaggerrakschlacht. The opening scenes recreate with real skill the atmosphere of suspense before battle.

The play, incidentally, is well worth reading for its delineation of the German military mentality. Here are the dying words of a would-be mutineer who has after all distinguished himself in the fighting:

> "I've done good work firing, eh? –
> And I'd have mutinied well, too, eh? –
> But the firing was nearer our hearts, eh? –
> Ay, it must have been nearer our hearts".

After the Fians.
Oisein an déigh na Feinne (Ossian after the Fians) is a Gaelic proverbial expression. Ossian is reputed to have outlived his compeers, the Fingalian heroes.

Jousts of the Toppo.
Dante Inferno, xiii. 118-21. The fugitives in the Wood of the Suicides.

Ballad of the Simeto : This poem was spoken by James Grant as part of the Commentary for the television film, *The Dead, The Innocent.* 'Tomb for the Gael' - the accompaniment to 'Ballad of the Someto', composed by Ken Hyder for his folk-jazz group Talisker - can be heard on their LP *The White Light* (Vinyl Records, Vinyl VS009).

Ballad of Corbara : My intention in writing this poem has been largely to achieve the effect that several notable Italian films have to their credit namely, the recreation of the atmosphere of the campaign by re-producing fragments of all the many languages spoken in that extraordinary period. The ballad will be found to be packed with technical expressions relating to anti-partisan warfare in both Italian and German and there are two whole stanzas in Landser's colloquial speech.

However, just as the *fondo* of *Vivere in Pace* is Italian so the foundation of this ballad is Lallans: a flexible modern Lallans based on the language of the Perthshire uplands, an area where for three generations at least it co-existed with Gaelic.

Corbara was one of the great partisans of Emilia. The legend of his prowess is related over the whole province, and into the Tuscan Apennines. The Germans eventually captured, and shot him they then hung up his body in the piazza of Forlì. The bodies of his woman Inez (who was pregnant) and of his principal Lieutenant were exhibited along with his own.   (1944)

If the episode on which this poem is based seems larger than life, so in fact are most of the stories told about Corbara between the Faentina and the Futa Pass.

Tedeschi.	Plural of tedesco, the Italian word for German. Also means 'boorish', 'Mis-shapen' and 'uncouth'.
Biretta.	Make of revolver.
pineta.	Pine wood.
die lustigen Hanoveraner.	"The merry Hanoverians" (German folk song)
Rastrellamento	Anti-partisan operation.
Du faehrst etc.	"You make for Faenza, I'll stay down here. We'll put the bandit Corbara in the bag right away.
Kraeder.	Motor-bikes
Kastanien.	Chestnut trees.
Dort ist er.	There he is.
Senta, etc	"Listen! Are you mad? … Surrender … Resistance is useless".
Dolmetscher.	Interpreter.
Sau-itacker.	Sow Italian
Kaninchen.	Rabbit.
Tedescacci	Accio in Italian is an ending signifying repulsion or hatred.
Deckung etc.	"Cover!" "On you go!" "Is the bitch in league with Satan?" "What's up with you?" "Are you going to let the bastard escape?"
Schnapp ihn	"Catch him!"
moribondo.	Dying man.
Sangue – Lupo – Uragano – Fulmine.	(Blood, Wolf, Hurricane, Thunderbolt) Battle names of partisans.

Eightsome Reel: Danced with the Sixth Gordons in Perugia. Tune: Kate Dalrymple.

Ballad of the D-Day Dodgers: This is my version of a Ballad which was circulating among the "8th Army scroungers" at the time.

Ballad of the Big Nobs: Taken up and Sung by the Eighth Army c. September 1942.

Ballad of the Banffies: I adapted a version which I heard spoken early on in 1944 and supplied the tune for it and it was taken up by the troops.

Requiem for the Men the Nazis Murdered: The thrilling violence of this poem in German is hard to recapture in English. We are not used to such strong stuff. The anti-Castlereagh broadsheet technique had not been much in evidence in Britain during the broad-bottomed era of Baldwin and Chamberlain: instead, we had the unvirile political badinage of the thirties. The Blitz, however, seemed to make it plausible even to bourgeois communists that British civilization could not remain protected for ever, and Alamein should have done the same for their counterparts in Cairo.

This was the sort of period when (the *Song of Roland* puts it succinctly): 'Païens ont tort et Chrétiens ont droit'. Fuernberg was a young Sudeten German poet who called a gun a gun and vengeance vengeance and he should not have difficulty now in finding hearers.

Somebody in the Eighth Army had a typescript of Fuernberg's poems and I translated some of them.

My Poems: I began to translated the Fuernberg poems in 1942. In the original, this poem is in rhymed verse. I have not attempted rhyme because of having to wrench the meaning. It's direct enough as it is. Also – so great a harm have our neo-Romantics done us – a rhymed translation would sound too artificial.

Lament for the Son: This is part of a long prose poem, here re-cast in verse, written by Govoni after the death of his son, Aladino, a partisan of Italy, who was one of 335 hostages shot by the S.S. under Kappler in the Ardeatine Caves, 24 March 1944.

Poem for Silvano: Written in the gardens of the Maadi Club, Cairo, May 12th 1942.

To Hugh MacDiarmid: This was written at Merano, in the south Tyrol (Italy) in the autumn of 1945. I was sitting thinking about MacDiarmid. The more I thought, the more I was puzzled.

The John MacLean March: Tune: traditional, arranged by myself. This version was transcribed from my own singing by the late Francis George Scott. It was first sung by William Noble at the John MacLean Memorial Meeting in the Saint Andrew's Halls, Glasgow, 9th November, 1948 and was specially written for that gathering. This was later described by Morris Blythman (Thurso Berwick) as "the first swallow of the Folk Revival".

Brosnachadh: Incitement to Rise.

Song of the Gillie More: Among messages of fraternal good wishes exchanged during Scottish-Soviet Friendship Week, at the height of the Cold War, was one 'From the Blacksmiths of Leith to the Blacksmiths of Kiev'. This song was published by the Associated Blacksmiths' Forge and Smithy Workers' Society to commemorate that event.

Glasclune and Drumlochy: The poem is, as it were, an echo of old warfare, as it still remotely pulsates in the folk memory. The "clannish confine" lies in jagged outline across Scottish history. I was thinking also, of course, of the millennial internecine conflict of humankind. The sung part of the poem is the ballad pastiche, and is in italics. The tune is a variant of 'Cam ye by Atholl?'.

Floret Silva Undique: The wood is flowering all about. In the travellers' cant, *darkmans* means *night* and *The kinchin's bara* means *the child is good* (i.e. willing).

Jokers abounding: Peter Duval Smith whom I first met at Cambridge produced the first BBC broadcast of the *Elegies*. *Brought to the ring* echoes Wallace's words to the Scots army just before the Battle of Stirling Bridge: "I have brought you to the ring, now you must dance". *Jouk the wuddy*: dodge the gallows.

Rivonia:

baaskap: white domination
keerie: club, cudgel
Amandla Umkhonto we Sizwe: power to the spear of the Nation.

Epistle to Mary: This was written to Mary MacDonald, wife of Fionn MacColla, on receiving an invite to the 21st birthday party of the School of Scottish Studies in 1972. At that time there was a scare, blown out of all proportion by the local press, about muggings on the Meadows. Hence, the referrences to Young Niddrie Terrors etc.

To Stuart – on his Leaving for Jamaica: In March 1972, the poet and novelist Stuart MacGregor left for Jamaica where he was to take up a temporary medical post. As a student at Edinburgh University in the 1950s, he had been a vital driving force in the early days of the Scottish Folk Revival. He was tragically killed in a car crash less than a year after arriving in Jamaica. This song is, of course, a Burns pastiche, to the tune of *The Silver Tassie*.